RESUME FACTORY

Writing Resumes for the 21st Century

By L F Peterson Ph.D.

Dr. Lawrence Peterson

Table of Contents

Introduction

Traditional resumes are starboard lights on a ship; they only illuminate the past. An effective document is forward looking. It includes not merely what you have done, but what you can do. Effective resumes illuminate the future. Once a career designation is chosen this new format can be built and trimmed like a well-directed ship to achieve its destination. The more closely your background and qualifications compare to the needs of the organization, the greater the frequency of offers. No matter how worthy your preferences, companies are motivated to fulfill their own needs. I call this process "self-interest psychology." Dale Carnegie build an institution on this approach when he said we can make more friends by being interested in others (companies) than by being interested in ourselves. Effective resumes are the indispensable ingredient to offers and career success for the following reasons:

Today's sophisticated wage earner has a low tolerance for being underutilized, particularly when peers are regularly changing jobs and receiving more money. Corporate mergers, acquisitions, divestures, staff reorganizations, downsizings, and corporate bankruptcies have decreased job security. There are now 7 billion people on the planet competing for attention. The need to stand out mandates the adoption of a specialized marketing device to obtain interviews. Positions traditionally requiring applications are now insisting on resumes to prescreen applicants and minimize wasted interview time. We do judge a book by its cover. An organized, professionally written resume produces a greater number of interviews. This means more job opportunities in less time and at less expense.

A psychiatrist once asked a patient how many telephone poles it took to reach the moon. The savvy patient responded it took only one pole if it were long enough. It takes only one good resume to land a rewarding position if properly written, directed and backed by an effective interview. A mere 3% return is considered a favorable response rate for direct mail. Well-written resumes can generate as high as 90% response if properly targeted. Personnel Departments encourage resumes formatted like applications because "fill-in-the-box" formats are easy to screen and file. Traditional resumes follow the Procrustes Syndrome named after the legendary robber who captured travelers and confined them to his bed of iron. Tall travelers longer than the bed had their limbs lopped off; short travelers were stretched to fit. Just as the bed served as the standard for Procrustes, resumes have remained the standard for millions of job seekers who volunteer to be underutilized because they have not adopted a better approach. Inside this handbook the reader will find the raw materials to create resumes for virtually every imaginable occupational area, from entry level to six figure incomes.

As a compliment to this handbook, consider reading, Transformational Job Strategies for Getting the Job you Want, Lawrence Frederick Peterson Ph.D., available on Amazon Kindle.

CHAPTER ONE

A thorn by any other name is still a thorn.

THE FIRST STEP INVOLVES IDENTIFYING THE PROBLEM

We live in an information society and the mail is still considered the least expensive means for communicating to companies we are looking for work. The single greatest shortcoming of resumes today is their conservative, autobiographical portrayal of prior work experience. Autobiographical formats resembling applications are simple to create and read, but are also the easiest to reject because they fail to motivate employers to grant interviews. The average job seeker mails out hundreds of old-style resumes in attempting to persuade a few decision makers to respond. Since resumes are the first step to securing an interview and rewarding offer, creating an effective resume is the most important project you will ever undertake.

Resumes are intended to accomplish two goals. First, resumes create an initial impression. Second, resumes serve to open doors to increased opportunity. Once an impression is created, it is difficult to change. This can be a tremendous service or disservice to the job candidate. A small group of psychologists once decided to investigate the significance of initial impressions in the mental health field by acting out a series of mental disturbances to gain admittance to mental hospitals. After being diagnosed by attending psychiatrists, the psychologists stopped pretending and began acting normally. As predicted, no matter how normal their subsequent behavior, their actions were always perceived within the context of the original diagnosis. In short, they were still perceived as mentally disturbed. This experiment clearly demonstrates the power of first impressions and why many resumes fall flat. Fortunately, positive impressions are also difficult to change in what is called the "halo effect." If an employer likes a candidate, they tend to exaggerate the candidate's strengths while underestimating the candidate's weaknesses. This handbook is written to help job candidates create resumes encouraging employers to exaggerate your strengths and thereby grant you interviews.

The first step in facilitating favorable employer response is to change the way you look at resumes. Why is it over the last few years tremendous advances have been made in marketing to successfully move billions of dollars' worth of products and services; yet, resumes continue to look pretty much the way they always have? Perhaps because resumes are not perceived as strategic marketing documents! Since the average employee changes jobs every 2.7 years, the one area sorely in need of technology is career development. Forget thinking of a resume as an application for work. Resumes are brochures that represent potential services for companies.

You are initiating a direct marketing campaign whenever you mail your resume to companies and successful marketing companies have invested millions of dollars in determining the most efficient means for ensuring consumer response. Why not apply their hard earned wisdom to your job search? Consumers are influenced by benefits because benefits represent the opportunity to gratify basic consumer needs. Traditional resumes make the mistake of listing features instead of benefits. In essence, traditional resumes document what you have done in hopes the employer will associate similar benefits for their firm. What if opportunities exist that are dissimilar to your existing background? In contrast to traditional resumes, strategic marketing documents offer organizational benefits representing opportunities for gratifying employer needs. Want more response from your resume? Design it around basic employer needs.

One method marketing companies use for identifying consumer needs is through the science of demographics compiling statistics on marriages, births and salary ranges, because purchasing preferences can be derived from mining data. Whenever you purchase a product from the local supermarket statistics are being compiled from electronic cash registers and subsequently sold to marketing companies. What you purchase is useful in determining what new products to introduce as well as what kinds of marketing campaigns work best in your area. When job candidates use this approach, hiring decisions can be inferred from data concerning the size of companies, level of sales, number of employees, product or service, location, whether in a growth cycle or a downsizing trend, potentially new technology and more. For example, if you are mailing your resume to a small company, you would want to show your diverse ability to multi-task and wear several hats in your summary of qualifications.

An important question all marketing organizations ask is, "Who is the target audience?" Similarly, job candidates need to ask, "Who can best advantage from my services?" It is critical to understand companies are motivated to fulfill organizational needs, not applicant preferences. Selling benefits to companies involves the principle of "self-interest." Avoid placing emphasis on your past when writing your resume. Include provisions for what you intend to do for a company and watch how quickly they respond with interest.

PUT YOUR BEST NAME FIRST

Every detail of your resume represents an opportunity to unconsciously influence your reader. The popular adage, "You never get a second chance to make a first impression," is particularly applicable to your name, address and phone number which communicate more information than you realize. Research has shown first names can influence school grades, corporate promotions and salaries regardless of personal effort or intelligence. Use formal names instead of nicknames or juniors, which promote stereotypical responses. For example, "Micki" is too familiar. Consider using Michele on your resume.

If you dislike your first name, use an initial and your middle name i.e., F. Robert Williams instead of Fred Robert Williams. Using junior i.e., Frank B. Bigelow, Jr. implies adolescence or the fact you stand in the shadow of your father. You can leave junior off of your resume while still including it on legal documents. Remember, resumes are brochures, not applications. The use of credentials differs with the kind of position you are going for. Credentials are generally placed under education instead of after your name unless the job calls for them. For example, Jack R. Hennin C.M.C. indicates a Certified Master Chef, the highest recognition in the trade. Jack R. Hennin M.B.A. is less appropriate for a personal resume because it suggests placing greater importance on academic background than business acumen. The M.B.A. degree is acceptable for a business resume mailed out to clients, just as C.P.A. is acceptable for accountants looking for new business. If seeking a job, consider placing the M.B.A. under education where it can serve as a surprise in what is called, "reverse snobbery."

Your address can also bias readers. A house number has more prestige than an apartment number suggesting you do not possess adequate finances to purchase your own home. The unconscious belief you lack investment power can unconsciously convince employers you will work for less. If you must use an apartment number try, "123D" which could imply you might own a condominium instead of "123 Apt. D," which shows you rent. Avoid Post Office Boxes.

Good
ROBERT B. THIGPIN
1150 N. Mountain Upland, CA 91786
(714) 949-0000

Too Informal
BOB "Bobby" THIGPIN 1150 N. Mountain Upland, CA 91786
No Phone

Low Prestige
Bob Thigpin
1150 N. Mountain, Apartment #4 Upland, CA 91786

Desperate
BOB B. THIGPIN, JR.
ADBA THE TREE DOCTOR P.O. Box 111 City of Industry, CA 91220 (714) 949-0000 Work Number (714) 949-0699 Answer Mach. (714) 949-0002 Neighbor Phone

Although email addresses are becoming commonplace, they can also appear informal. Avoid chat addresses. Answering machine numbers and answering services are to be avoided because of their impersonal nature. In the modern world most of us have a smart phone keeping us current. If the company wants to interview you they will make the effort to call you in the evening. A work number, even if employer permission is granted, suggests a misuse of company time or misplaced loyalty. The thought process is, "how can he accept calls while at the office?" If the employer believes you are taking advantage of your current firm, what will they conclude about your next company? Listing too many phone numbers suggests desperation. Avoid using 800 numbers or fax numbers.

Dr. Lawrence Peterson

Ms. Alexis Jones
1121 W. Pointer Avenue, Trent, MI
(619) 223-9988
Ajones@gmail.com

The size of your name is also important. A large name can project confidence; a huge name suggests conceit. The name, address and phone number is grouped together for reader convenience. Women can minimize bias by using the title, Ms. instead of Mrs.

JOB TARGETS THAT SOAR

After the name, address, and phone number, the objective is the first and foremost element of the resume and serves as the guiding principle upon which the rest of the document is built. Even if the objective is left off, the document still has a hidden objective by virtue of the order and direction of information. In borrowing a hunting analogy, a shotgun will hit something just as a large number of unfocused resumes will get some response. Focused resumes fetch the highest number of responses when they offer benefits strategically geared to the needs of the company. The most effective objective is one expressing employer benefits subsequently reinforced throughout the document for a cumulative effect. "Sales Manager seeks new opportunities for enhanced account development," is an example of an objective easily reinforced in a summary of qualifications, job description and cover letter. Reinforced qualifications quickly become ingrained in the employer's mind. Emphasizing what we want or hope to receive in the objective is a common mistake in resume writing. When the objective promises a well-defined employer benefit, the rest of the document can be written to support the introduction. Think of the Objective as a "thesis statement" in which the entire composition is encapsulated in one sentence.

Terse
General Sales Manager

Concise
General Sales Manager seeks new opportunities for the development of sales, repeat business and qualified referrals.

Good
Marketing professional with a track record for enhancing account revenue seeks new challenges in a customer-oriented firm.

Average
Sales Representative with diverse product experience seeks affiliation with a progressive electronics firm.

Poor
Salesman seeks position with a growing concern so that background, interest, and opportunity for personal growth can be utilized for future career advancement.

Overkill
Come and get it! Dynamic Sales Representative with awesome closing ability seeks new interpersonal horizons to ameliorate extant transactions as well as cultivate the augmentation of new account revenues.

Confused
Jack of all trades but master of none seeks an opportunity to apply diverse background from the school-of-hard-knocks to the hands-on needs of a potential company.

Desperate
Neophyte seeks an entry level position and will do anything to get a job.

Weird
Puff the magic computer hack rides again. Can slay any hardware of software dysfunction quicker than the Black Knight.

RESUME OBJECTIVES

Objectives can encourage immediate interest because benefits are promised at the onset. Objectives can also be utilized to convey precise information about the kind of position you seek, as long as they do not swell to epic proportions. Consider a list of objectives for different positions.

Administrative Assistant with medical support expertise seeks new challenges in a supportive office environment where insurance and collections competence can fulfill account objectives.

Architect with commercial design exposure seeks affiliation with a growing university to utilize prior project experience and familiarity with educational funding requirements to further campus building objectives.

Bookkeeper with strong computerized receivables and payables experience desires affiliation with a progressive manufacturing organization to expedite auditing and accounting transactions.

Certified Public Accountant with diverse industrial exposure seeks affiliation with an international manufacturing firm desiring new account validation in the United States.

Certified Welder with extensive offshore fabrication experience seeks challenging field assignments requiring underwater welding expertise.

Computer Programmer with C, Perl, AJAX, and Fortran language proficiency seeks analyst position with software firm to further program writing objectives.

Construction Specialist with fast-tracking commercial and residential experience seeks Superintendents position with a growing builder to expedite project initiatives.

Counselor with psychiatric training seeks affiliation with a private mental health facility to facilitate the care and recovery of adolescent substance abusers.

Data Processing Specialist seeks responsible position with a Law firm to provide overall computer and system management support for improved reporting and data retrieval.

Education Coordinator with Elementary School seeks position in a secondary education setting to facilitate bi-lingual and ESL instruction.

Engineer with South America exposure seeks affiliation with a leading research firm so hands-on field experience can be applied to the successful location of oil.

Fireman with EMT Paramedic Certificate seeks increased responsibility as a Fire Captain to promote the efficient response to ongoing emergency assignments.

Fleet Car Salesman with high volume track record seeks new challenges with an existing dealership desiring additional sales in the commercial truck market.

Hotel Attendant with front desk and catering experience seeks affiliation with a successful hotel chain to facilitate hospitality objectives.

Inspector with multi-story commercial renovation experience seeks position with building contractor to expedite quality assurance objectives.

Jailer desires affiliation with a state directed detention facility to complement on-going incarceration policies and initiatives.

Manager with multi-chain responsibility seeks affiliation with a growing retail organization so that merchandising expertise can promote product turnover and profitability.

Motorcycle Racer with competitive international exposure

seeks sponsors willing to invest equipment and technical expertise in exchange for marketing exposure derived from successful race results.

Nurse with Emergency and Operating room experience seeks technical position in Pediatrics to foster effective treatment and care of premature infants.

Optometrist seeks affiliation with growing retail lens distributor to apply both technical and social skills to the development of new sales, repeat business and referrals.

Production Technician with wiring loom experience seeks quality assurance position with a growing electronics firm requiring soldering certification and computer test board experience.

Quality Assurance Supervisor desires immediate affiliation with a progressive fastener organization demanding strong detail orientation and technical competence.

Real Estate Sales Representative with residential home and financing experience seeks affiliation with a local builder to promote new home sales.

Sales Representative with diverse product experience and international connections seeks affiliation with a European manufacturer to promote sales in the American market.

English Teacher seeks affiliation with a challenging school district needing strategic classroom management skills for GATE student achievement.

Trainer with diverse industrial exposure seeks affiliation with a growing manufacturer who will benefit from curriculum development and presentation skills.

Underwriter with seasoned troubleshooting skills desires affiliation with a progressive mortgage banking firm to expedite loan processing initiatives.

Warehouseman with shipping and receiving experience seeks new challenges with a growing transport organization requiring automated equipment and material handling expertise.

Employer interest is captured by offering benefits at the onset. For example, if you are a police officer your main benefit is to preserve law and order. Managers maximize capital and human resources. Sales Representatives open new accounts and service existing accounts. Each classification has its own features and benefits. The question to ask when seeking a new position is, "What service is most beneficial to the company?" After identifying the benefit, turn the benefit into an opening statement. Qualifications are more idealistic and forward looking than experience. We are qualified to perform services we may never have had the opportunity to implement with other companies.

CHAPTER TWO

FORMATS THAT WORK

Job turnover statistics verify long-term employment is quickly becoming a concept of the past. Colleges are opting for part-time teachers to keep costs down. Companies are using consultants and temporary office personnel to accomplish work objectives without assuming responsibility for sustained staff overhead and health benefits. Futurists suggest the worker of tomorrow will occupy several positions in response to rapid changes in the employment sector. As the workplace changes nine-to-five jobs give way to short-term employment assignments and computer terminals logging on to new projects everywhere in the world. This trend translates into good news for job candidates sufficiently flexible to adapt their resumes to new job descriptions.

Diversity of work assignments will minimize burnout. Equally important will be a leveling effect on income since compensation will be derived from several sources instead of one. On the cautionary side, resumes emphasizing past work accomplishments will become even more useless when it comes to fetching important interviews. Why? Because one of the major by-products of new technology is the creation of new job opportunities frequently inconsistent with prior work experience. Since traditional resumes emphasize prior employment they will become less practical in the modern market. When employers are confronted with traditional resumes they tend to think in terms of apples and apples; your last assignment is compared with openings in similar areas.

If no opening exists your resume is filed. A major stumbling block in emphasizing the past involves stereotypical responses. New resumes emphasize company benefits over prior employment so job candidates gain access to new job opportunities based on what can be done rather than what has been done. The typical approach when reading resumes is screening. Resumes can become loaded documents encouraging discrimination. An effective resume is strategically written to minimize unfavorable bias. Since traditional resumes are written along an application format, the one area quickly encouraging bias involves the use of dates.

DATES

Dates can raise immediate flags because of potentially harmful information they disclose. Listing the date you graduated from college allows readers to calculate your probable age. Including all jobs you have held since High School also discloses information about your age. Why volunteer information potentially working against you? The number of years you have worked for a company creates bias if the sum total is substantial. Twenty years with one company can imply you are relatively set in your ways. The question is, "Why now do you want to change?" The old adage, "One year's experience twenty times," comes to mind. In contrast, documenting your short tenure with a company also raises questions regarding why you looking for another opportunity after recently accepting one.

Traditional resumes list the day, month and year of employment. Breaks in service are easy identified and create unfavorable bias even if the break was as brief as a single month. Recent research shows resumes showing breaks in employment service are less frequently responded to. The application format allows any deviations in employment to conspicuously stand out. Why lose interviews? A more effective means for documenting dates with companies is available.

List companies with the number of years worked is one alternative. Consider the following samples:

Five years' experience as Manufacturing Manager providing strategic troubleshooting initiatives to accomplish challenging fabrication initiatives. The preceding example focuses on the number of years instead of the start and stop dates potentially encouraging Personnel Managers to use their slide rules.

Present: Manufacturing Manager responsible for promoting quality and operational efficiency through specialized research and development programs. In this example you merely state you are presently working for a company. How long is not as important as how good. The employer may ask you how long you were with the company. You are in a stronger position to explain long or short tenure in person than to ask a document to do it for you.

Another alternative utilizes dates of most recent positions while referring to previous experience as just that:

Present: Sales Manager for a progressive chemical material company with profit and loss facilities throughout the United States. Previous experience includes working as Field Engineer for a chemical factory in New Jersey.

Three years is generally considered an acceptable length of service for many jobs and can be listed without bias.

Present: Purchasing Agent for progressive metal fastener firm serving the aerospace industry.

2012 - Present: Purchasing Agent for progressive metal fastener firm serving the aerospace industry. This example implies you just accepted the position and raises red flags.

Age bias must also be considered when including dates on your document. Including thirty years of work experience can convince employers they are dealing with someone who is looking to retire on the job. The Occam's razor approach (the simplest explanation serves best) is more effective. Stating you demonstrate over twenty years' experience in a particular field is sufficient to impress anyone. Pride for technical achievements is laudable and understandably you want an employer to respect the number of years you have practiced your craft. Employers believing they are dealing with a Mayflower Pilgrim seldom ask for interviews. Effective resumes do not raise concerns because employers seldom take time to investigate. Resumes generally do not go back more than ten years because experience prior to ten years is considered old hat.

REARRANGING WORK HISTORY

Senior executives have long understood the disadvantage in being overly specific when listing companies worked for or amount of time spent in positions. They realize background, qualifications, and level of responsibility are what counts. Skillful writing maneuvers readers to predetermined conclusions, something marketing takes for granted. Omit unrelated experience raising questions the document cannot answer. If your most recent position is not relevant to your objective, consider reversing or rearranging your work history to create a logical format congruent with the position sought.

For example, you left plastics for a position in real estate and now want back into plastics. You could list your plastics experience first and your real estate experience last, or leave the real estate experience off altogether. If you were successful in opening accounts in real estate and are pursuing a sales position in plastics, the document could present a convincing argument on behalf of your general sales ability. Consider listing prior plastics experience first in the objective and summary of qualifications. An effective resume is a brochure of what you can do for a potential company. By starting off with "real estate," in the preceding example the reader may never get beyond the first job description before rejecting the document because of bias. Minimize bias by listing the most significant elements of your background and qualifications first. Downplay unrelated experience which only serves to distract or confuse the reader.

MILITARY EXPERIENCE

Armed Forces experience once indicated freedom from future military commitment. In today's climate, resumes generally do not include military service unless it is the most recent vocation or played a significant occupational role potentially marketed for a civilian job. Technical training derived from the Armed Forces can translate into civilian positions. Unfortunately, artillery experience has few applications in the civilian sector and would serve to distract the reader from considering you for commercial opportunities.

Military service is generally left off of the resume unless pertinent to the position or no other experience is available. If lacking civilian experience, translate military leadership into management terminology. Consider how rigid discipline of the military can translate into dogmatic management practices currently being deemphasized in today's business climate. If you are still drawing attention to military accomplishments after having worked in the civilian sector, the emphasis raises questions concerning your business acumen. Such a practice might suggest you feel the need for supporting documentation because your actual work experience is weak.

THROW OUT THE KITCHEN SINK

Pertinent information is critical to persuade employers to make hiring decisions; including too much information leads to reader apathy. Eliciting an employer's appetite is critical to getting offers. The quickest means for ensuring employer motivation is to document what is in it for them if they bring you aboard. The fact you belonged to the Glee Club or played Varsity Football is extraneous; as would be your Eagle Scout status. Similarly, affiliations like the American Rifle Association do not add to the marketability of the document and would serve to unfavorably bias a reader who might favor gun control. Likewise, including personal information about religious affiliations does not strengthen the document, but certainly can raise questions and bias. There are laws against discrimination. What the law actually prevents is employer's telling you the real reasons they did not ask for an interview.

MARGINS ET AL

Generous margins are clean and make for easy reading. Magazines and newspapers have successfully used the linear format for years because they understand readers like convenience. Resumes incorporate a manuscript format with at least 1" margins top and bottom, and 1 1/4" margins on both sides. In this instance, less is more. Written material is centered between margins and avoids typewriter graphics that serve little purpose but to distract readers.

BULLETS

o Bullets (small o's) are much cleaner than asterisks. They are effective for highlighting specific points for the reader. If used too frequently; however, they lose impact.

o Small o's, if used, are to be left blank for a cleaner appearance. Resist the temptation to fill them in. There are provisions in certain word processing programs to insure that information following the o's aligns with the rest of the text to preserve right margin justification. Program manuals typically include such information in the index.

Short, single-spaced entries can also be portrayed without bullets and still get the job done nicely. Avoid overusing bullets in an endeavor to create an outline resume. After all, a resume is an opportunity to show the employer you can write.

CENTER STACK HEADINGS

Resume formats can center stack headings or left margin flush for convenient reading. Justified type looks neat and polished thereby enhancing the professionalism of the document. We do judge a book by its cover. The overall appearance of the document encourages interest and employer follow-up. Although truncated (shortened) sentences have traditionally been accepted, resumes conforming more closely to Standard English provide improved readability and flow. The desired effect is to focus the verbiage on benefits for the employer. Well-chosen words disappear into the background so employer opportunities jump out. A well-written resume looks simple until one sees the detail and thought behind the arrangement and wording. Poorly-written documents are painfully obvious, as their poor response confirms.

GRAPHICS AND PHOTOGRAPHICS

A resume is a marketing proposal. Inserting graphics into the document can effectively communicate ideas, but care must be taken to ensure the document does not become lengthy or resembling an advertisement. Effective brochures are notorious for distilling pertinent information into a few paragraphs. Pie graphs, histograms, and illustrations can be judiciously included as long as the quality is intact. Fancy items like directive hands, arrows and flowery borders only clutter the document. Word-processing software produces attractive resumes with strong marketing appeal. Resumes generally include four pages.

A title page strategically arranges your name, address and phone number so it can show through a window of a notebook if chosen. A brief objective can be included at the bottom of the page. For dramatic impact, the name can be created using bold print.

John Work
1121 East Cambridge Avenue
Claremont, CA 91701

The second page in an executive notebook presentation is reserved for the cover letter which introduces the document while reinforcing the summary of qualifications. The third page consists of the summary of qualifications and education. The fourth page lists pertinent work history and professional affiliations. Photographs have long been avoided in resumes because of potential discrimination, but photographs have been known to add a personal touch. Any hook you can etch in the employer's mind is a point in your favor. I am reminded of a job candidate who wrote their resume along a cartoon format because they were going for an art designer's job. The strategy landed them the interview and the job.

PERSONALITY PROFILES

Executive management style and emotional temperament influence corporate dynamics. Corporations are beginning to utilize a variety of psychological instruments to measure organizational climate and staff compatibility. Including a psychological profile at the end of the resume is a unique way of convincing a key decision maker they are making the right decision when it comes to staff dynamics. It also serves as a marketing tool to focus the employer on desirable personality traits. Consider the following when developing your resume.

Management personality tendencies:

Problem solving and troubleshooting.
Making quick decisions.
Getting immediate results.
Freedom to effect change.
Opportunity to propose recommendations.

New and varied activities.
Difficult and challenging assignments.

Sales personality tendencies:

Making a favorable impression.
Contacting clients and generating enthusiasm for products.
Verbalizing product attributes for greater sales.
Opportunity to verbalize and present proposals.
Freedom from over control and excessive detail.
Recognition, popularity and prestige.
Participatory management.

PAPER AND PRINT

Even the kind of paper and print style elicits reactions from the reader. Avoid inexpensive paper suggesting you place little importance on presenting your qualifications. Garish colored paper enables you to stand out in the wrong way. Quiet elegance is the best choice. For the best image and professional impact, paper should be at least 60 pound bond. It can include parch tones in such colors as crème, blue, gray, ivory and white. Offset Vellum by Simpson is an excellent paper for most purposes. One of the predominant colors for resumes has been beige so consider adopting a different color to stand out from every other candidate mailing in their resume. Paper demonstrating a 25% rag fiber content conveys solidity. The importance of presentation is demonstrated by Education. Sheep Skins (diplomas) are printed on the finest parchment and placed in quality frames. Similarly, executive presentations often utilize quality notebook covers with windows to affect a similar result. The paper should complement the color of the notebook. The industry standard for print is 12 pitch, Arial. Elite is appropriate when printing your cover letter because it resembles handwriting. Dot matrix printers cannot compare with Laser printers because of their draft appearance. The color of business print is still black.

If the resume looks average what conclusion might the employer make? Why look like other job candidates whose resumes get filed? Standard letter size is the only acceptable dimension for a professional resume. This size can also be achieved by folding an 11" x 17" page in half, with the name on the front and resume information inside. A border on the cover formalizes the document but can also be distracting. The fold serves as a pocket to insert the Cover Letter. A folder is generally used by candidates going for over $50,000 in annual salary; a notebook for candidates above $100,000.

CHAPTER THREE

A resume is a short summary long on experience.

PROFESSIONAL EXPERIENCE

Resumes ensure flow and integrity by following a specific writing sequence. The first step is deciding a suitable career objective. If answering an advertisement, the objective is the position offered. After the objective comes a summation of qualifications. After the qualifications comes experience. The cover letter emphasizes items in the summary of qualifications for emotional impact. When writing the resume, job candidates find it easier to first list their experience and from their experience develop a summary of qualifications. Resumes are written in shorthand and can deviate from complete sentences.

Resume writing steps:

Objective. 2. Summary of Qualifications. 3. Professional Experience. 4. Cover Letter.

Employers are more company oriented than title oriented. Resumes place the name of the company first and the position second. Traditional resumes underlined the position. This is not only grammatically incorrect, but places more emphasis on the title than on skills and abilities. What if the title is misleading or restrictive? Effective resumes include the title within the narrative so it is taken for granted. In short, understatement can be advantageous. Consider the following:

AMERICAN WRITING SERVICE, Upland, CA

2005 - Present: Staff Writer for progressive, multi-million dollar career development organization with affiliated locations throughout California and Arizona. Responsibilities include performing intake interviews for the creation of strategic marketing documents geared to upwardly mobile executives.

PROFESSIONAL MARKETING DYNAMICS, Claremont, CA
Present: General Sales Manager for leading marketing organization providing assistance to small to medium sized retailers in the Inland Empire. Responsibilities include promotional advertising, demographic analysis, merchandising and staff sales training for improved performance, productivity and volume through stand-up presentations and video feedback.

Effective resumes prioritize experience to increase employer response. When pertinent skills come first the employer can scan the document and still come away with sufficient information to pick up the phone and request an interview. The job title is followed by responsibilities and activities. For managers, this often means the number of facilities, departments directed, location or specialization, the product or service, and annual sales volume if appreciable. Any special instruction and training would go under education. The entire thrust of the job description is to inform the reader of benefits to his company.

Management Hierarchy of Information:

Company Name
Job Title
The number of employees
Kind of product or service
Operating competence
Manpower proficiency
General duties
Pertinent accomplishments

Position requirements

Examples:

JACKSON COMMERCIAL, INCORPORATED, Los Angeles, CA
Present: Production Supervisor with directional responsibility for a staff of 500 involved in the manufacture of commercial lighting devices for aerospace applications. Operating activities include profit and loss accountability, budgeting and forecasting in conjunction with the implementation of effective cost reduction strategies. Routinely perform master scheduling and manpower planning to maximize capital and human resources. General duties include conducting management meetings to foster compliance with operational objectives. Recent accomplishments display successful plant reorganization improving production through-put by 300%. Position necessitates strong technical skills in addition to the ability to function effectively within the confines of strict government specifications.

RESEARCH PROFESSIONALS, INCORPORATED, Chino, CA
Present: Vice President of Program Development for leading scientific organization involved in creating ceramic materials demonstrating zero resistance at room temperature. In addition to coordinating a $35 million dollar budget, also secure funding from investors through extensive informational interviews and key presentations at corporate meetings. Interface with leading scientists in securing specialized equipment to further test initiatives. Conduct interviews with media representatives to explain research implications. Developed and promoted a program investigating barium oxide derivative for increased funding.

Technical Hierarchy of Information:

Company Name
Job Title
The number of employees (if applicable)

Kind of product or service
Kinds of equipment or processes
Technical competence
General duties
Pertinent accomplishments
Position requirements

Examples:

TECHNOLOGY PLASTICS, Pomona, CA
Injection Molding Specialist responsible for coordinating the efforts of five Mold Makers and affiliated technical personnel making of high quality molds for consumer product applications. Routinely compare job progress with blueprints and design specifications to ensure quality and customer satisfaction are maintained. Interface on a daily basis with production in a research and development capacity to find means for making molds function more effectively and faster in a forced production environment. Accomplishments include initiating a scrap recovery program that pared 25% off of the purchase of raw plastic materials. Position necessitates extensive machine shop exposure in addition to the ability to interface effectively with technical personnel.

TITLE PROPERTY MANAGEMENT, San Dimas, CA
Present: Property Manager for this highly visible management organization with operational responsibility for over 500 units. Activities include advertising, credit verifications, lease negotiations, receivables and collections. Routinely coordinate maintenance and repairs with particular attention given to safety and quality assurance. Successfully initiated a neighborhood watch program to minimize thefts. Launched a rent incentive program promoting timely tenant payments.

JACKSON CONSTRUCTION COMPANY, Cucamonga, CA
Present: Construction Superintendent with responsibility for

over 300 custom residential tract homes in the Rancho Cucamonga area. Position necessitates strong project management skills and seasoned budgeting proficiency. Interface with Inspectors and municipal personnel for permits in support of client change orders. Extensive knowledge of the building trades enhances quality assurance initiatives for improved customer service and conformance to state and federal building regulations.

TERMINAL ANNEX CORPORATION, Los Alamitos, CA
Maintenance Foreman responsible for routine, preventative and corrective maintenance on paper binding equipment. Since published materials are time dated, position necessitates the ability to function effectively in pressure situations to meet tight scheduled deadlines. Have initiated a computerized inventory control reserve for critical parts to ensure maximum uptime and system integrity.

HILLSDOLL HIGH SCHOOL, Fullerton, CA
Certified Teacher responsible for providing quality instruction to students from Freshman to Senior Student Body encompassing differing ages and learning capabilities. Curriculum topics include English, Writing and Grammar in addition to computer training. Instruct both College Bound and GATE students in conjunction with developing specialized learning materials and presentations. Other activities include in-service training to facilitate new teachers with the acquisition of effective training and classroom management strategies.

CHAPTER FOUR

THE SUMMARY OF QUALIFICATIONS

If a career objective is included in your resume, the Summary of Qualifications emphasizes facts complementing this objective. Objective and SOQ work together like foundation and house to impress potential employers of the benefits they will receive when they hire you. Resumes are strategically written to include what companies want to hear without resorting to exaggeration or deception. By positioning powerful attributes (hooks) first and general characteristics last, the employer digests your best points immediately. You never get a second chance to make a powerful first impression.

The proper emphasis is important in securing the right kind of interview. When going for a supervisory position, too much accent on technical skills could result in reader confusion. A supervisor focuses on management abilities further supported by technical competence. References to staff training, scheduling, and employee performance evaluations are key to building a logic stream. The higher we ascend the corporate ladder, the less nuts-and-bolts oriented the resume. As a CEO with Profit and Loss responsibility it is not necessary to demonstrate the coordination of specific activities in every company department. Senior executives are sought for their vision and leadership skills.

WIDENING VISTAS

The SOQ not only allows a prioritized, focused documentation of skills and abilities, it appeals to a wider market. Most employers compare apples with apples when it comes to resumes. They assume the most recent position is indicative of what we do best. Since Resumes are forward looking, summarizing qualifications avoids tunnel vision and thereby afford greater appeal and impact. Apples and oranges are both fruits, so resumes elaborating commonalities widen market appeal.

Management and marketing skills are applicable to virtually any product or service. The beauty of the SOQ is that it lists things we "can" do. College attendance qualifies graduates to perform a wide range of activities, even though work experience is temporarily lacking.

For example, communications training in interpersonal psychology can be applied to stand-up sales presentations for enhanced product visibility and account revenue. This example suggests a tie in with sales, despite the job candidate not having actual experience in sales.

Award recognition at the World Robotics Symposium effectively demonstrates research and development expertise as well as practical problem solving competence with sophisticated electromechanical configurations is an example showing hands on experience.

Hands-on laboratory experience in micro-particle physics can readily be applied to superconductivity research and development initiatives is yet another example of actual experience projected into other another affiliated research field.

Prior business experience and recent academic exposure to the latest management theories promises improved performance and productivity in virtually any manufacturing environment. In this example, the term "promises" says it all.

EXAMPLES OF QUALIFICATIONS IN SPECIFIC CAREER FIELDS

ACCOUNTING

Accounting positions necessitate well-developed analytical skills along with strong attention to detail. It is also critical the resume show the basic principles and procedures of accounting practices. The ability to read, interpret and draw conclusions from accounting reports and documents is a strong marketing statement. General Ledger, payables, receivables, financial statement preparation, bank reconciliations and auditing are also important elements to include in the resume. Since computerized accounting and payroll programs are becoming popular, proficiency with computer programs and spread sheets is a valuable asset.

Auditor

Over 13 years' experience in auditing and financial analysis with comprehensive knowledge of accounting QS 9001, ISO 14001 and TS 16949 procedures.

Extensive troubleshooting and problem solving ability complemented by sound account resolution skills and an excellent understanding of taxation and auditing.

Coordination of nationwide audits including company premium audits of over $2 million.

Expertise in budgeting, forecasting, lap top field audits experience and statistical sampling.

Seasoned analytical decision making ability with concern for detail and accuracy.

Business and personal tax return competence complemented by cash flow management skills.

Solid knowledge of government regulations for compliance and precision.

Thorough understanding of insurance rules and regulations.

Comprehensive tax research and planning skills, as well as payment, dividend plans, coverage's, special values and state exceptions.

Demonstrated proficiency in individual, partnership, and corporate taxes.

Oral and written report presentations to management including the ability to initiate policies and procedures for enhanced fiscal control.

Staff training in ASQ supported by outstanding interpersonal communication skills for enhanced motivation and organizational commitment.

Participant in Tax Compliance Management Program (TCMP) for corporations and individuals.

Capable of functioning effectively in pressure situations to meet scheduled deadlines.

Bookkeeper

Over 15 years responsible experience in bookkeeping backed by extensive administrative and account management expertise.

Bookkeeping exposure encompasses General Ledger, financial statement preparation, bank reconciliations, receivables, payables and tax reports.

Extensive troubleshooting and problem solving skills allow for rapid diagnosis and workable solutions to account and collection dysfunctions.

Demonstrated ability to read, interpret and draw conclusions from accounting reports and documents as well as improve financial reporting times.

Can readily audit existing accounts and funds while preparing payroll records, invoices, time records and requisitions.

Analytical skills include project tracking and prioritization abilities to coordinate a variety of on-going assignments.

Strategic planning expertise is supported by the ability to function effectively in pressure environments to meet scheduled deadlines.

Controller

Corporate Controller seeks increased responsibility in a challenging environment where background can be applied to the efficient satisfaction of organizational objectives.

Summary of Qualifications

o Computer skills with Excel/Lotus, Word, QuickBooks, PowerPoint, Option Tracker, Quark Express, ATB, ProFx Tax & Trial Balance, Lacerte, Gosystems Tax, ExacTax.

o Over 20 years progressive experience in accounting with extensive corporate management responsibility.

o Comprehensive background in the budgetary control of a multi-state chain of retail outlets.

o Extensive troubleshooting and problem solving skills to rapidly analyze and resolve personnel and internal fiscal control issues.

o Demonstrated ability to perform scheduling and manpower planning activities in addition to conducting performance reviews to foster productivity.

o Sound project management capability exemplified in the development of the corporate Southwest Region Distribution Center.

o Seasoned analytical decision making ability competence to maximize and sustain favorable operating profits.

o Consistently promoted to levels of increased responsibility due to management and administrative achievements.

o Capable of functioning effectively in pressure situations to meet scheduled deadlines while providing critical leadership for goal accomplishment.

o Familiar with corporate procurement and sales practices in conjunction with budgeting, forecasting, and long range planning functions.

o Facilitate dealer and subcontractor interfaces for enhanced rapport and cooperation to meet corporate objectives.

o Outstanding oral and written communication skills including stand-up presentation proficiency.

o Staff training and development abilities include strong motivational skills for increased productivity.

Controller-General

Controller seeks increased responsibility in a challenging environment where background and experience can be applied to the efficient satisfaction of fiscal objectives.

Summary of Qualifications

o Over 12 years responsible experience in accounting backed by extensive administrative and management proficiency.

o Administrative skills include profit and loss responsibility, budgeting, forecasting, long range planning, and projections.

o Comprehensive accounting expertise in several organizational settings supported by strong personnel proficiency.

o Able to initiate policies and procedures for enhanced fiscal control and cash flow.

o Extensive initial start-up experience for enhanced expansion and organizational integration.

o Sound troubleshooting and account resolution skills are further supported by an excellent understanding of finance, law, marketing, taxation, auditing, and computers.

o Demonstrated ability to read, interpret and draw conclusions from accounting reports and documents as well as improved financial reporting times.

o Solid knowledge of tax and government regulations for compliance and precision.

o Able to function effectively in pressure situations to meet scheduled deadlines.

o Computer literate with demonstrated application for management reporting and fiscal accountability.

o Interpersonal relations abilities for enhanced rapport and cooperation with clients and co-workers.

Cost Analyst

Certified Management Accountant with over 13 years progressive experience satisfying accounting and finance objectives with a track record for expediting project efficiency.

Comprehensive auditing proficiency includes system evaluations with regard to the identification of strengths and weaknesses with recommendations for enhanced control.

Extensive troubleshooting and problem solving skills pertinent to such government regulations as DAR, FAR, CAS and DCAM.

Demonstrated expertise with public vouchers and progress payments backed by the ability to teach corporations how to obtain funds from government sources.

Operating competence includes budgeting and forecasting, in addition to scheduling and manpower planning to maximize capital and human resources.

Supervise auditing personnel pertinent to such applications as Forward Pricing Proposals, Overhead Claims, Labor and Overhead Bid Rates, and Employee Compensation, to Progress Payments, Disclosure Statements and Delay Claims.

Seasoned personnel skills include policy and procedure initiation and training applicable to auditing, report writing and basic organization.

Conduct stand-up presentations with Controllers, Cost Estimators, Company Presidents, and affiliated finance personnel.

Capable of reviewing and evaluating accounting systems with regard to internal controls and overall costing systems for enhanced compliance with stated objectives.

Computer proficiency includes Excel/Lotus, Word, Quick-

Books, PowerPoint, Option Tracker, Quark Express, ATB, ProFx Tax & Trial Balance, Lacerte, Gosystems Tax, Exac-Tax.Lotus, Multimate, Statistical Sampling, and a variety of business software to access record bases, perform follow-ups and generate critical reports.

Dr. Lawrence Peterson

CPA

o Certified Public Accountant with several years responsible experience in accounting and auditing backed by extensive administrative proficiency.

o Comprehensive accounting expertise includes full-service bookkeeping, from General Ledger and budget preparation to Financial Statements and Inventory Control.

o Demonstrated ability to reconcile all accounts, execute wire transfers and bank transactions, maintain petty cash, vendor invoices and 1099 files.

o Extensive troubleshooting and problem solving skills supported by an excellent understanding of finance, business law, taxation, and actions required for audit compliance.

o Demonstrated accounting expertise in diverse environments complemented by strong proficiency in fiscal data analyses.

o Sound knowledge of government laws and regulations for effective compliance backed by seasoned analytical decision making ability.

o Budget preparation experience for grant proposals related to federal funding, in addition to proficiencies auditing federal, state and private grant funding systems.

o Can function effectively in pressure situations to meet scheduled deadlines while maintaining an emphasis on detail and accuracy.

o Strong background in credit and collections relative to determining credit limits, analyzing customer financial statements, and enhanced cash flow management.

o Familiar with such computer applications QuickBooks, Axapta, eBusiness Suite, MAS 500, Solomon, ACCPAC, RSD,

IFPS, FOCUS, LOTUS 1-2-3 and ALWAYS.

o Demonstrated ability to perform scheduling and manpower planning activities in addition to providing for performance reviews to foster productivity, commitment and accuracy.

o Capable of coordinating special meetings and industry shows as well as training programs.

o Outstanding oral and written communication skills to recommend or initiate changes in policies and procedures for enhanced financial control and operational efficiency.

o Interface with upper management and affiliated financial personnel to maintain fiscal integrity.

Credit and Collections

o Over 11 years' experience in credit operations with computer expertise with Titanium ORE, SimplicityCollect, CreditPoint, CollectPlus, PIMS, eCollections, AdvantEdge, LiveVox and more.

o Familiar with creative collection procedures to minimize defaults while maintaining positive customer relations.

o Demonstrated negotiation proficiency with attorneys to avoid litigation as well as interface competence with Credit Bureaus and Consumer Agencies.

o Sound analytical decision making abilities backed by experience with Fortune 500 accounts to approve and determine credit lines, clarify leasing clauses and resolve credit disputes.

o Extensive account troubleshooting and problem solving skills pertinent to receivables, credit reports, personal asset auditing and client repayment procedures.

o Capable of performing timely diagnostic analysis with particular attention to prevention for enhanced operational performance.

o Familiar with such computer systems as CRT and IBM to expedite data processing objectives and maintain precise documentation and monitoring of accounts.

o Can achieve targeted DSO objectives without impacting sales growth while keeping bad debt write off to a minimum.

o Seasoned interpersonal communication skills for enhanced rapport and cooperation with management, co-workers, clients, and credit and collection agencies.

o Consistently able to maximize personnel resources through strategic hiring, training, performance appraisals and leadership skills.

o Comprehensive staff supervision abilities include scheduling, manpower planning, and auditing for conformity to stated policies and procedures.

o Capable of assisting in effective staff training and development programs for enhanced performance, productivity and commitment.

Financial Administration

Several years' responsible experience in accounting backed by Controller expertise for enhanced operating and organizational control.

Comprehensive Profit and Loss accountability along with supervision proficiency for the maximization of capital and human resources.

Extensive troubleshooting and problem solving skills for the rapid diagnosis and remedy of account deficiencies.

Demonstrated accounting expertise includes General Ledger, payables, receivables, inventory control and financial statement preparation.

Experience computing direct labor, general and administrative overhead rates and have assisted in bid proposal preparation and government audit bid rates.

Seasoned management skills pertinent to weekly cash budgets to determine appropriate cash disbursements.

Consistently able to initiate effective administrative policies and procedures for improved control and compliance.

Capable of reviewing internal control procedures in conjunction with assigning and reviewing staff performance, productivity and accuracy.

Familiar with computerized accounting through such programs as Lotus, DAC Easy, First Choice, AceMoney, Account Xpress, ICash, Quicken and QuickBooks.

Well-developed oral and written communication skills in addition to staff training and development abilities.

Personnel skills include hiring, performance reviews and motivational strategies for enhanced rapport and cooperation.

Financial Planner

Progressive experience with municipal bond and underwriting activities to foster significant account development and referrals.

Comprehensive marketing proficiency includes extensive networking to secure valuable information utilized for effective buy and sell options.

Account troubleshooting and problem solving skills relative to audits, settlements and reconciliations for such applications as equity and fixed income products.

Demonstrated operational competence pertinent to profit and loss accountability, budgeting, forecasting, projecting and portfolio development.

Sound analytical decision making abilities in conjunction with effective interpersonal presentations to foster new business as well as retain key accounts.

Frequently serve as a resource person for retail sales desks and registered representatives regarding currency and availability of specialized bonds.

Consistently recognized for outstanding sales performance and product knowledge while demonstrating a popular following with prior accounts.

Capable of interfacing with syndicates and marketing available bonds to potential buyers while demonstrating familiarity with NASD, SEC and MSRB rules and regulations, particularly from the underwriter's perspective.

Well-developed oral and written communication skills supported by computer proficiency with Bloomberg and Lee Data System, eMoney, MasterPlan, NaviPlan, PFP Notebook and more.

Dr. Lawrence Peterson

Internal Revenue Agent

Comprehensive tax research and planning skills.

Extensive troubleshooting and problem solving ability.

Demonstrated proficiency in individual, partnership, and corporate taxes.

Sound account resolution skills supported by understanding
of taxation and auditing.

Solid knowledge of government regulations for compliance
and precision.

Able to initiate policies and procedures for enhanced fiscal
control and cash flow.

Seasoned analytical decision making ability with concern for
detail and accuracy.

Participant in Tax Compliance Management Program (TCMP)
for corporations and individuals.

Capable of functioning effectively in pressure situations to
meet scheduled deadlines.

Familiar with indirect methods of arriving at gross receipts.

Computer literate - acquainted with Lotus 123, Dbase, Word
and topical accounting programs.

Tax Auditor

Issue levies on real property and bank accounts as well as wage garnishments and earnings withholding orders.

File liens on real and personal property and issue warrants to seize and sell real and personal property including liquor licenses.

Research civil, penal and U.S. Bankruptcy codes in addition to revenue and taxation codes.

Prepare and research civil cases for offices of Attorney General, processing criminal cases for District Attorney.

Work in conjunction with the IRS, Franchise Tax Board, and Employment Development Department.

Coordinate work efforts with U.S. Bankruptcy trustees and attorneys pursuant to resolving claim objections, inadequate disclosure statements and reorganization plans.

Analyze mark up and gross profit percentage figures relative to profit and loss statements.

Trace source documents from income and expenses to recorded figures.

Evaluate and compare figures from recorded journals to general ledger through to financial statements.

Test source data and apply to statistical sampling to audit reports.

Write audit reports with commentary decisions of auditors. Participated in oral panels and chaired oral panel for entry level professional candidates.

Function as in-service training instructor for tax compliance and law.

Provide direction and serve as resource for other represen-

tatives in collection cases and criminal prosecution assignments.

ADMINISTRATION

The basic difference between Management and Administration has to do with the Organizational Chart. Management is a line function. Managers generally contribute directly to the company's product or service. Since management requires continual supervision to ensure performance is maintained, managers are often too busy to take care of the growing mountains of paperwork. Therefore, staff functions necessitate professional administrative personnel to support busy line managers. An Administrator typically handles things instead of people. A Procurement Administrator might interface with outside vendors and sales representatives to negotiate purchase agreements. A Warranty Administrator with an automobile manufacturer functions in a liaison capacity between the manufacturer and dealership to expedite payment of warranty claims. Since support functions are indirect and therefore considered overhead, effective resumes include any related cost reduction experience which would reduce direct and indirect costs. It would also be effective to include the ability to interface with line personnel to promote overall operational efficiency.

Administrative Manager

Over 13 years' experience in administration supported by extensive policy and procedure implementation to foster organizational efficiency.

Expertise in planning, implementing, and coordinating special and routine projects, including report documentation to further production initiatives.

Analytical problem solving abilities allow for expedient solutions to both organizational and operational dysfunctions.

Sound union interface skills include collective bargaining negotiations for improved rapport and cooperation between exempt and non-exempt personnel.

Auditing and inventory expertise encompasses both semi-annual and monthly inventory reporting, reconciliations, determination or recounts, and special investigations.

Computer proficiency includes inventory, billing, routing, and tracking activities to expedite procurement and distribution initiatives.

Methods improvements and work simplification expertise includes cost reduction abilities to significantly maximize capital and human resources.

Shipping, receiving, and warehousing expertise supported by material handling proficiency to expedite the systematic movement and filling of goods.

Scheduling, manpower planning, training and staff development expertise in support of line management to complement production objectives.

Interface proficiency with outside vendors and sales representatives to negotiate purchase agreements and procure necessary equipment and supplies.

Financial Administration

Several years' responsible experience in accounting backed by Controller expertise for enhanced operating and organizational control.

Comprehensive Profit and Loss accountability in addition to basic supervision proficiency to maximize capital and human resources.

Extensive troubleshooting and problem solving skills for the rapid diagnosis and remedy of account dysfunctions.

Demonstrated accounting expertise includes General Ledger, payables, receivables, inventory control and financial statement preparation.

Experience computing direct labor, general and administrative overhead rates and have assisted in bid proposal preparation and government audit bid rates.

Seasoned management skills pertinent to weekly cash budgets to determine appropriate cash disbursements.

Consistently able to initiate effective administrative policies and procedures for improved control and compliance.

Capable of reviewing internal control procedures in conjunction with assigning and reviewing staff performance, productivity and accuracy.

Familiar with computerized accounting and data processing system applications through such programs as Lotus, Quick-Books, eMoney, Daceasy and First Choice.
Well-developed oral and written communication skills in addition to staff training and development abilities.

Personnel skills include hiring, performance reviews and motivational strategies for enhanced rapport and cooperation.

Contract Administration

Six years of responsible Administrative experience supported by increased proficiency in the expedient delivery of contracted supplies and services.

Comprehensive analytical decision making abilities backed by prioritization skills for enhanced organizational efficiency.

Extensive troubleshooting and problem solving skills to rapidly identify and correct operational dysfunctions.

Demonstrated ability to function effectively in pressure situations to meet scheduled deadlines.

Interface proficiency with suppliers and subcontractors in the procurement of supplies, equipment and services for optimal cost effectiveness.

Team player recognized for leadership qualities as well as outstanding personal performance in the satisfaction of operational initiatives.

Interpersonal skills for enhanced cooperation and commitment are supported by well-developed oral and written communication proficiencies.

Computer literate with D-Base, Word, Excel/Lotus, Quick-Books, PowerPoint, Option Tracker, and Quark Express.

ADMINISTRATIVE SPECIALIST

This category can be used for general office and sometimes field opportunities where field representative, clerk, office support or secretarial is not appropriate. Typically the Administrative Specialist deals more with special projects or operational activities requiring organizational and prioritization skills. There could be staff responsibility. Always include the ability to handle multiple projects simultaneously; frequently customer service concerns, troubleshooting and problem solving. If typing, shorthand or technical (maintenance, sales or marketing) expertise is not a strong suit, then this is the category for you.

Administrative Specialist

Several years' progressive experience in administration supported by strategic policy and procedure initiation for enhanced operational and organizational efficiency.

Strong prioritization skills to coordinate a variety of ongoing projects simultaneously.

Seasoned organizational competence in addition to a strong attention to detail for precise record keeping and documentation.

Sound troubleshooting and problem solving skills to rapidly diagnose and correct operational dysfunctions.

Demonstrated ability to function effectively in pressure situations to expedite project objectives while meeting scheduled deadlines.

Sound staff skills include hiring, evaluating, training and motivating personnel for conformance to stated policies and procedures.

Consistently able to apply leadership experience and interpersonal communication proficiency to instructional trainings for enhanced rapport and cooperation with clients and co-workers.

Capable of working effectively within budget parameters to facilitate project initiatives as well as control expenses.

Interface with management, key decision makers, co-workers and individuals from diverse cultural backgrounds.

Able to work effectively individually or as a team for enhanced operational efficiency.

Well-developed oral and written communication skills are further supported by stand-up presentation proficiency.

Dr. Lawrence Peterson

AEROSPACE

Defense contractors are involved in proposals, prototype development, manufacturing and contract administration. Engineering candidates in virtually all categories are critical to aerospace operations, whether electronic, research, or manufacturing oriented. Reference to MIL-STD's (military standards) is important, because defense contracts necessitate strict adherence to rigid engineering specifications. Costs are important and audits are mandated both internally and by the Defense Department. Progress payments are often made solely on approvals at specific manufacturing phase. Experience with contract interpretation and negotiation is important since an average sized project may fill rooms with supporting documentation. Any interface with vendors and subcontractors is marketable because many items are farmed out to maintain schedule and to minimize cost. Since projects require security, candidates possessing a security clearance should list its type and level on their resume.

Analog and Digital Design Engineer

Electronics Engineer seeks increased responsibility in a challenging environment where background can be efficiently applied to the satisfaction of design objectives.

Summary of Qualifications

o Design theories include Fourier series for signal analysis - as well as Fourier, and Fast Fourier Transforms for design and analysis of discrete systems in addition to knowledge of Laplace Transforms for design and analysis of analog systems.

o Hands-on experience in digital communication systems, wave shaping circuits, and computer interfacing as well as with the partial design, fabrication and debugging of transistor tester circuits.

o Worked with design draftsmen to develop engineering sketches into finished drawings while generating new drawings pertinent to new system designs, changes and modifications for implementation into the production environment.

o Developed test procedures for new design modifications to test equipment in addition to developing equipment calibration procedures.

o Extensive troubleshooting and circuit diagnosis proficiency to the component level supported by practical experience in circuit modification for test station applications.

o Experience with component layout, diagnostic checks, and system performance evaluations.

o Sound design skills backed by blueprint, wiring schematic, and technical proficiency to conform to military specifications.

o Scheduling proficiency includes procurement manifests, in-process analysis, correlation interface, and Gantt charting for expedient project completions.

o Able to effectively interface with Mechanical Engineers, Technicians, Contract Administration, Document Control, Draftsman, Procurement, and Vendors.

o Knowledge of a variety of computer languages including C, AJAX, Perl, Java, PHP, Python, and VB Net.

Composite Manufacturing

Technical specialist seeks increased responsibility in a challenging composite manufacturing environment leading to the satisfaction of organizational objectives.

Summary of Qualifications

o Over 25 years' experience in the design and production of composite assemblies for advanced aeronautical systems.

o Comprehensive background developing of manufacturing tooling and processes for assurance of design production.

o Extensive troubleshooting and problem solving skills to correct identified defects during manufacturing to optimize production efficiency.

o Demonstrated master scheduling and manpower planning proficiency to maximize capital and human resources.

o Consultant to Design Engineering on composite structural members and bonded components to facilitate the manufacture of unique designs.

o Sound knowledge of Mil-Specs and applicable standards associated with composite materials and production processes for enhanced productivity and quality assurance.

o Capable of performing manufacturing capability, engineering production and trade-off studies in support of design for cost minimization.

o Familiar with DoD aeronautical system general proposal requirements to provide extensive inputs for major system procurement.

o Interface proficiency with management, subcontractor, and customer personnel to facilitate program performance.

o Well-developed oral and written communication skills in

conjunction with stand-up presentations expertise.

o Staff training and development of manufacturing engineers for enhanced utilization of human resources.

Design Specialist

Progressive experience in mechanical design engineering for effective project development.

Comprehensive design and redesign experience, from concept through production.

Extensive troubleshooting and problem solving skills.

Demonstrated proficiency in proposal development.

Sound cost reduction through alternate designs and parts simplification.

Experience with 3D modeling software as well as DesignSoft.

Proficient with ISO 9001, 14000, 10005, ANSI A1117 and Z97.

Familiar with PERT, CPM, and Gantt charting for scheduling.

Excellent understanding of machine shop practices, including tooling and fixtures.

Inspection and non-destructive testing expertise, including vibration tests and isolation tests.

Knowledge of casting relative to design applications.

Interface proficiency with vendors, electrical, machine shop, test equipment and the program office personnel.

Outstanding oral and written communication skills.

Able to adapt quickly to new organizational settings.

ENGINEERING
Industrial Engineer

Industrial Engineer seeks increased responsibility in a challenging environment where hands-on experience can be utilized to satisfy production and manufacturing objectives.

Summary of Qualifications

o Extensive hands-on experience in production and manufacturing environments with a track record for significantly augmenting fabrication and assembly efficiency.

o Operational competence includes budgeting, projecting and forecasting in addition to follow-up for enhanced compliance with project requirements.

o Comprehensive experience in developing standard data for use in establishing production standards, in addition to proficiency with work measurement and work simplification.

o Competent with machine cycle times, machine thru-put, operation sequencing charting and manpower loading in addition to master scheduling and manpower allocation.

o Extensive troubleshooting and problem solving skills to rapidly diagnose and remedy operational and organizational dysfunctions.

o Familiar with product design and new product manufacturing introductions necessitating changes in assembly processes, routing modifications and tooling alterations.

o Sound interface skills with customers, upper management, and affiliated departments and agencies for improved operational response and efficiency.

o Capital justification experience with emphasis on return on investment includes tooling requirements, plant and work station layouts for enhanced manpower utilization and cost reduction.

o Capable of functioning as a resource person to provide valuable technical assistance to affiliated project personnel, including reviewing engineering designs and tooling concepts for production feasibility.

Quality Assurance Management

Quality assurance management, methods, organization, product liability, and manufacturing productivity.

Extensive working knowledge and experience with such quality systems as MIL-Q-9858A and MIL-I-45208.

Mechanical design and manufacturing engineering.

Technical quotation and proposal preparation.

Field inspection and customer communications.

Familiar with all NDT testing procedures.

Strong technical written and oral communication skills.

Ability to make significant contributions to cost reduction.

Implementation of Statistical Process Control (SPC).

Introduction of geometric dimensioning and tolerance systems.

Implementation of non-conforming materials policy, corrective action procedure and M.R.B.

Introduction and justification of computer-aided design and reporting system, as well as computerized discrepancy system.

Preparation of metallurgical and Q.A. procedures, company standards specifications, including design acceptance and test procedures.

Dr. Lawrence Peterson

On-site supervision of inspection projects in Canada, Australia and U.S.A.

Quality Engineering

Over 15 year's responsible experience in Quality Engineering backed by sound management and administrative expertise.

Comprehensive exposure to "life-cycle" program development, resulting in enhanced system integration with diverse manufacturing processes.

Fiscal troubleshooting and problem solving skills is supported by demonstrated budgeting and forecasting proficiency.

Sound personnel skills encompass hiring, coordinating and motivating staff members exhibiting diverse backgrounds.

Comprehensive experience with ground and airborne systems includes heavy software emphasis and compliance with MIL-STD-1553B.

Consistently able to expedite large and unique project initiatives to effect the greatest return on investment.

Capable of interfacing with Research and Development, Marketing, Engineering and Production to further project initiatives.

Familiar with Human Engineering requirements pertaining to computer driven "auto versus manual" workstations for pilot efficiency.

Multi-million dollar project expertise to pragmatically address Military and multiple government requirements within stated contract parameters.

Department of Defense Clearance with EBI.

Electronics Management

Several years' responsible experience in management backed by electronic proficiency in complex environments.

Comprehensive budgeting, forecasting and projecting expertise with a track record for exceeding production requirements.

Extensive technical troubleshooting and problem solving skills to quickly diagnose and remedy operational dysfunctions.

Demonstrated leadership qualities include interpersonal communication skills, labor relations, and staff appraisals for enhanced productivity, performance and quality.

Sound industrial engineering competence regarding time and motion studies, projection and operation charts, and time standards for enhanced through-put and projection performance.

Seasoned background in manufacturing includes quality assurance management, organization, product liability, and manufacturing methods for enhanced productivity.

Consistently able to develop and direct the production and distribution of specialized electronic products using understanding of manufacturing processes.

Capable of managing large projects as well as multiple programs of varied complexity and scheduled completion dates.

Familiar with such computer applications as Word, Lotus 1-2-3, and Graphix software.

Interface with Engineering, Quality Departments, Vendors, Purchasing, Human Resources and upper management for improved performance and productivity.

Facilitate staff commitment and cooperation through union negotiation expertise.

Well-developed oral and written communication skills.

Manager - General

Professional Manager seeks increased responsibility in a challenging manufacturing environment where background can be efficiently applied to satisfy mission objectives.

Summary of Qualifications

o Extensive management experience applicable to such operations in a Research, Development, and Production Engineering environment including Finance, Production Control, Manufacturing, Procurement and Marketing.

o Comprehensive profit and loss accountability includes budgeting, forecasting, projecting, inventory control and contract administration supported by a track record for efficiently operating within program budget parameters.

o Seasoned troubleshooting and problem solving skills from an operational and technical perspective to successfully expedite program initiatives as well as conform to military specifications and other contract technical requirements.

o Demonstrated bidding support as well as feasibility analysis to provide effective production recommendations for improved program performance and productivity.

o Sound interface skills with clients, suppliers and outside laboratories is supported by vendor negotiations and competitive price comparisons to maximize capital and human resources.

o Seasoned staff training and development proficiency in addition to strategic hiring and evaluating skills to promote productivity, performance and commitment to program objectives.

o Consistently able to function effectively in pressure situations to meet scheduled deadlines.

o Capable of initiating policies and procedures to expedite program cooperation while ensuring that stringent documentation requirements are complied with.

o Well-developed oral and written communication skills supported by stand-up presentation skills to key decision makers.

MANUFACTURING
Manufacturing and Production

26 years' experience in aircraft, missile and helicopter manufacturing and maintenance supported by production supervision proficiency.

Operational competence includes budgeting, projecting and forecasting in addition to follow-up for enhanced compliance with contractual requirements.

Extensive troubleshooting and problem solving skills to rapidly diagnose and remedy operational and organizational dysfunctions.

Familiar with product design and new product manufacturing introductions necessitating changes in assembly processes, routing modifications and tooling alterations.

Sound interface skills with customers, upper management, and affiliated departments and agencies for improved operational response and efficiency.

Familiar with DoD general proposal requirements to provide extensive inputs for major aeronautical system procurement.

Seasoned ability to function effectively in pressure situations to meet scheduled deadlines as well as handle multiple projects simultaneously.

Consistently able to assume positions of increased responsibility through leadership abilities and team building proficiency.

Comprehensive background in personnel training programs for enhanced operational efficiency and production.

Capable of functioning as a resource person to provide valuable technical assistance to affiliated project personnel.

Facilitate operational integrity through policy and procedure initiation as well as staff training to maximize human and capital resources.

Material handling proficiency with an emphasis on safety, quality assurance for CAL-OSHA compliance.

Department of Defense Security Clearance with EBI.

Procurement

Over 15 years responsible experience in procurement supported by extensive contract administrative expertise.

Comprehensive expertise in bidding, proposal evaluation, negotiations, source selection presentations and cost/price analysis.

Extensive troubleshooting and problem solving skills complemented by a sound understanding of Federal Acquisition Regulations and other government procurement regulations.

Exceptional organizational skills for increased efficiency and productivity backed by cost reduction expertise through planning analysis, negotiations and timely deliveries.

Demonstrated ability to review program requirements regarding subcontractor efforts with particular attention devoted to budgetary constraints.

Establish requests for subcontractor RFP's and transmit to qualified bidders as well as review minority business requirements.

Capable of assembling a survey team to review potential subcontractor systems for ability to perform to subcontract requirements.

Establish and monitor subcontractor performance such as status reporting and subcontract reviews in accordance with stated requirements in addition to reviewing make-buy decisions.

Recognize and report on subcontractor problems to ensure resolution and shipment of deliverables (hardware and SDRL software) on schedule and cost expenditures within established budget.

Interface proficiency with upper management, key decision makers, vendors and technical service personnel.

Quality Control

o Over 10 years progressive experience in a Quality Control environment supported by strong management expertise for improved project efficiency.

o Comprehensive background with mechanical and electrical inspection processes including required item configuration, conformance with specified dimensions and wire routing to specified schematics.

o Able to determine item compliance with characteristics using non-destruct test methods such as dye penetrant and mag particle inspection.

o Troubleshooting and problem solving skills for the efficient resolution of operational deficiencies.

o Demonstrated Inspection acceptance responsibility for incoming materials, in-process and completed article shipment.

o Support programs for strict compliance with MIL-Q-9858A Quality Systems requirements and MIL-I-45208A Inspection requirements.

o Sound background in Quality Engineering with responsibility for engineering, manufacturing, test, and customer interface for resolving quality problems.

o Extensive Material Review Board experience to insure proper disposition of hardware and investigation of cause of discrepancies to ensure effective corrective action.

o Consistently utilize sampling plans for cost reduction with minimal risk of accepting defective parts per MIL-Std-105 and MIL-Std-414.

o Thoroughly familiar with acceptable level of workmanship standards at close tolerances.

o Capable of supervising non-exempt Quality employees to provide timely resolution of quality problems and continuing flow of in-process hardware.

o Perform Quality Data Analysis associated with rejected parts in MRB to prevent reoccurrence of discrepancies.

Systems Analyst

Programmer/Systems Analyst seeks increased responsibility in a challenging environment where background and experience can satisfy systems objectives.

Summary of Qualifications

o Responsible experience in systems analysis and design backed by large project exposure and comprehensive hardware and software expertise.

o Extensive troubleshooting and problem solving skills to analyze dysfunctions and make recommendations.

o Demonstrated knowledge of business practices and system effectiveness, including design implementations.

o Customer data gathering to define specifications.

o Supervision proficiency which includes planning and schedule work assignments for others.

o Establish project controls to insure the effective use of resources within established time frames, as well as step-by-step instructions for efficient machine utilization.

o Capable of writing computer programs using current practices and developments for custom applications.

o Have authored system documents as well as trained others in the operation of specific systems.

o Experience supervising, coordinating and performing test schedules, test data requirements and validations.

o Facilitate the development and execution of system implementation plans, including time estimates, and progress reports on assigned projects.

o Extensive knowledge of programming and systems techniques for mid-range electronic computers.

Dr. Lawrence Peterson

o Working knowledge of organizational methods, financial management and record keeping.

AIRCRAFT-AIRLINES

Aircraft jobs range from building and flying the planes, to flight maintenance, freight handling and arranging for passenger flights. Flying a commercial jet requires years of experience in a co-pilot capacity. Therefore, the number of flying hours is a critical element included in the resume. Working on planes requires technical expertise and certification. Freight and cargo handling may involve compliance with F.D.A. and U.S.D.A. regulations as well as experience with Customs clearances and seizures, export declarations and controlled substance licenses. Flight Attendants are hired for their interpersonal skill, appearance, and poise in functioning effectively with difficult passengers.

Airline Support Specialist

o3 years' experience in airline operations.
oComprehensive understanding of airline support functions.
oExtensive troubleshooting and problem solving skills.
oDemonstrated ability to supervise others.
oSound customer relations skills.
oConsistently able to meet scheduled deadlines.
oCapable of assuming greater responsibility.
oCounter operations, lost and found procedures, ramp operations, and load planning.
oPerform extensive customer relations,
oFacilitate enhanced organizational efficiency,
oComputer - CRT skills relative to reservations.

Mechanic

oAirframe and Powerplant Certificate.(See A&P for detailed SOQ)
oExtensive experience in aircraft maintenance.
oHave established procedures for aircraft maintenance.
oDemonstrated ability to perform aircraft inspections.
oNumerous recommendations for increased aircraft safety.

oStaff training and development abilities.
oDoD Clearance with EBI.
oNumerous courses in aircraft related procedures.
oAdapt quickly to new organizational settings.
oTroubleshooting and problem solving skills.
oAbility to work with all tools for aircraft repair.
oAward for significant aircraft part cost reductions.
oAward for outstanding aircraft maintenance service.

Avionics Technician

o 3 years' experience hands on experience in avionics.

o Extensive electrical troubleshooting skills.

o Able to read all schematics and electronic symbols.

o Demonstrated expertise with wire bundle repair.

o Comprehensive skill with oscilloscopes, multimeters, time domain reflectometers.

o Experience with electronic countermeasures, 2A5X3C, AOE-39, ALQ-144, ALQ-157, as well as computer navigations, ARC-182, ARC-102.

o Bench experience with ARN-84's and helicopter subassemblies,

o Also adept with starter igniter systems,

o Familiar with radar altimeters and flight control electronics, as well as integrated flight guidance systems, S.C.A.S.

Airframe and Power Plant Mechanic

Experienced A & P in both military and civilian environments with particular emphasis on management activities.

Background expertise in Transport aircraft encompassing C-141, A and B models, C-5, A and B models and all models of the C-130.

Also experienced with general aviation type aircraft such as single and multi-engine Cessna in addition to familiarity with Beechcraft, Piper and the Cessna Caravan (turboprop).

Knowledgeable of all aircraft emergency and fuel systems complemented with sub-system expertise with structural, electrical, hydraulics, pneumatics, instrument, environmental and diverse military configurations.

Comprehensive Engine expertise includes Pratt and Whitney, TF-33 andPT-6, General Electric, TF-39, Allison, JT-56 familiarity as well as Continental and Lycoming reciprocating powerplants.

Prop experience encompasses McCauleys, Hartzells, Sensenich, Hamilton Standard.

Familiar with all maintenance and calibration requirements and procedures for major equipment, troubleshooting test units, torque wrenches, and tensionometers.

Expertise in all 50, 100, 1000, 5000 and 10,000 hour inspection requirements for assigned aircraft.

Computer literate with AT&T, Honeywell, Zenith, Sperry's and IBM interlink systems.

Well-developed oral and written communication skills with German proficiency.

Cargo

Cargo operations specialist seeks increased responsibility in a challenging shipping setting where experience can be applied to the efficient satisfaction of customer service objectives.

o Over 16 years' in cargo operations supported by understanding of import - export legalities.
o Extensive troubleshooting and problem solving abilities.
o Demonstrated supervision skills for enhanced staff motivation.
o Strategic freight handling decision making.
o Inboard and outboard handling, freight distribution and documentation.
o Perform cargo handling for Air New Zealand and Canadian Airlines International.
o Comply with all F.D.A. and U.S.D.A. regulations prior to shipment.
o Obtain U.S. Customs clearance for inbound and outbound freight.
o Present documents for export declarations and controlled substance licenses.
o Insure Customs seizures remain in custody.
o Coordinate loading structures via shipping manifests.
o Perform sales quotes and contract negotiation.
o Coordinate highest priority shipments for greatest revenue.
o Manage arrival of fruits with the U.S. Agriculture Department.
o Serve as liaison between broker and customer to expedite perishable warehouse goods.
o Shipping expertise with exotic automobiles.
o Packing expertise with produce, chilled meat and sea food.
o Dangerous goods separations with familiarity of radioactive goods and explosives.
o Initiate tracings to locate freight and arrange door to door shipping with outside suppliers.

Commercial Pilot

Commercial Pilot's license backed with ASMEL and Instrument ratings.

Familiar with both turboprops and turbojets pertinent to such general aviation executive aircraft as King Air, De Favilland, Lear and Citation.

Extensive troubleshooting and problem solving skills pertinent to airframe diagnosis and maintenance.

Capable of functioning in pressure situations to expediently satisfy operational requirements.

Interpersonal relations abilities for increased rapport with clients and co-workers.

Analytical decision making ability for precise cockpit control and flight integrity.

Consistently demonstrate strong organizational skills for increased efficiency, performance and productivity.

Comprehensive inspection and servicing proficiency relative to ground support equipment and aircraft preflight requirements.

Staff training, scheduling and manpower planning competence for the efficient utilization of human resources.

Strong oral and written communication skills backed by excellent record keeping.

Team player with the ability to adapt quickly to new organizational settings.

Flight Attendant

Flight Attendant candidate seeks increased responsibility where background and experience can be applied to expedite passenger objectives.

o Outstanding interpersonal skills for enhanced interface proficiency with passengers from all backgrounds complemented.

o Able to deal effectively with difficult people and function effectively in pressure situations for sound passenger troubleshooting and problem solving abilities.

o Well organized with a strong detail orientation for precise compliance with flight regulations and procedures.

o Possess airport operations exposure to expedite flight arrangements.

o Able to work independently or as part of a team for enhanced operational efficiency.

o Excellent photogenic appearance with modeling experience displaying a height of 5'6 and weight 115.

o Maintain physical fitness through aerobics and ballet.

Traffic and Transportation

Several years of responsible experience in management supported by a track record for significantly improving operational efficiency.

Comprehensive traffic and transportation expertise includes strategic expense control and budget awareness to maximize profitability.

Extensive troubleshooting and problem solving skills to rapidly diagnose and remedy operational and organizational dysfunctions.

Sound analytical decision making abilities supported by scheduling, master scheduling, manpower planning and manpower utilization to maximize capital and human resources.

Seasoned planning, implementing and coordinating expertise pertinent to routine and special project completions.

Demonstrated interface proficiency with management, key decision makers and affiliated personnel to further organizational policies and objectives.

Seasoned interpersonal communication skills with management and union personnel backed by stand-up presentation proficiency for enhanced cooperation and rapport in meeting forecasted goals.

Consistently able to function effectively in pressure situations to meet scheduled deadlines as well as to expediently handle crisis situations.

Capable of hiring, evaluating, training and motivating staff personnel for enhanced performance, productivity and organizational commitment.

Interpersonal skills to facilitate a team atmosphere and customer satisfaction are backed by the ability to interface with individuals from diverse cultural backgrounds.

Well-developed oral and written communication skills are supported by computer experience with SABRE, CARGOFAX, CLAS, AFIS, TRAC.

78

TRAVEL AGENT

Travel Facilitator seeks increased responsibility in a challenging environment where background and experience can be applied to the efficient satisfaction of organizational objectives.

Summary of Qualifications

o Several years' experience in the airline industry complemented with supervisory proficiencies.

o Outstanding interpersonal skills to facilitate a team atmosphere and customer satisfaction.

o Seasoned background in telecommunications, sales, marketing and special services

o Able to provide efficient itinerary planning and coordination for individual, group, and corporate travelers.

o Capable of expediting travel arrangements utilizing working knowledge of ramp, reservations, customer service and gate requirements.

o Familiar with domestic and international travel, fares, and tariff regulations.

o Sabre and Apollo computer proficiency.

o Extensive troubleshooting and problem solving skills.

o Possess strong decision making abilities, particularly in pressure situations.

o Qualified to fulfill a variety of challenging assignments.

o Outstanding oral and written communication skills.

o Staff training and development capabilities.

o Able to adapt quickly to new organizational settings.

ARCHITECTURE

Architecture requires engineering expertise, insight into construction processes, and well-developed design abilities. Work environments range from urban planning and residential to commercial and industrial. Although some architects work with new structures encompassing several stories, others involve themselves with remodeling's ranging from entire apartment buildings to small as a room addition. Architects require a license and strong familiarity with building design codes and regulations. They are often involved in proposal writing, bidding and contract negotiation prior to an award of a project. After award, they can monitor or directly manage the project. Computer literacy is critical in today's world of design, and CAD (Computer Assisted Design) familiarity is a valuable marketing tool, as is LOTUS proficiency when it comes to project tracking.

Architect

Over 19 years progressive experience in architectural project management pertinent to residential, commercial and industrial assignments including historical restoration, remodeling, and design from the ground-up through close-out.

Comprehensive project troubleshooting and problem solving skills maintaining strict compliance with stated regulations as well as quality assurance for enhanced client satisfaction and project efficiency.

Demonstrated negotiation expertise in addition to project fee analysis, proposal writing, contract administration and construction document production coordination.

Sound scheduling and manpower planning competence supported by specific work assignment delegation, performance evaluations and follow-up activities.

Seasoned document control includes change orders, clarifications, construction work authorizations, billing disbursements for consultants and all job close-out activities.

Consistently able to keep projects on track toward goals while coordinating with the Principal-in-Charge and other project mangers to maintain budgetary parameters.

Computer literate with CAD/CAM, Word and LOTUS for Windows to expedite drawings as well as track large projects.

Interface with the PIC/AIC to review and update the PICOST while acting as the office contact with all governmental agencies and other regulatory groups.

Staff training and development abilities to maximize capital and human resources.

AUCTIONEERING
Auctioneer-Automotive

Over 6 years' experience in auctioneering with a significant track record for facilitating bid transactions.

Extensive management proficiency backed by comprehensive automotive exposure.

Was involved in the purchase and development of a successful automotive auctioneering organization.

Experience establishing Fleet Lease, Arbitration, Collection and Detail Departments.

Sales and Marketing activities include advertising, promotions and account development with major automotive firms.

Profit and loss responsibility includes budgeting, forecasting, projections and cash flow analysis.

Strong scheduling abilities relative to transportation pick-ups, both cross country and local itineraries.

Initiated and managed special factory sales with Nissan, Mazda, Hundai and Dihatsui organizations.

Interfaced with Title Companies, approved credit and handled repossessions as well as Court proceedings when required.

Draftsman, AUTOCAD Operator.

Progressive experience in mechanical design engineering utilizing AutoCAD for effective project development supported by management proficiencies resulting in enhanced operational efficiency.

Comprehensive design and redesign experience includes change orders, updates, assembly and subassembly drawings, from concept through production using velum, mylar and AUTOCAD applications.

Extensive troubleshooting and problem solving skills pertinent to traffic flow, pipe, plumbing and electrical routing analyses, elevations, grading and landscaping.

Sound cost reduction through alternate designs and recommendations for design simplification include master scheduling for expedient operational control.

Interface proficiency with upper management, subcontractors, and customers to expedite project initiatives and ensure conformance to blueprints and project guidelines.

Well-developed oral and written communication skills include strict documentation and military specification conformance.

Staff training and development capability for enhanced motivation and commitment to project objectives.

AUTOMOTIVE SALES MANAGEMENT

(Sales and Marketing Specialist) or (Management specialist with sales and marketing proficiency) seeks increased responsibility in a challenging (automotive sales) environment where background and experience can be applied to the efficient satisfaction of organizational objectives.

Summary of Qualifications

Over 15 year's progressive experience in the automotive environment supported by Profit and Loss accountability, budgeting, forecasting, and projecting proficiency.

Sound record for facilitating dealership turnarounds to demonstrate a substantial increase in volume and profit.

Seasoned marketing abilities in such areas as advertising, in-store promotions, and multi media presentations.

Comprehensive business administration and finance skills for enhanced organizational efficiency and customer satisfaction.

New car inventory control expertise includes creating a favorable mix to maintain a 45-60 day turn.

Used car expertise includes buying, selling and wholesaling to achieve a 45 day inventory turn.

Comprehensive troubleshooting and problem solving abilities for increased business development and enhanced customer service index.

Finance proficiency includes negotiating with banks and other lending institutions to achieve favorable contract terms.

Demonstrated ability to augment sales through financing, insurance, and after market products.

Supervision proficiency includes staff training and development activities.

Computer literate to complement data processing and management reporting objectives.

Automotive Specialist

Technical engineering specialist seeks increased responsibility in a challenging automotive environment where background and experience can be applied to the efficient satisfaction of organizational objectives.

Summary of Qualifications

o Over 14 years responsible experience in automotive service supported by extensive profit and loss experience with positive results.

o Participative management orientation with particular emphasis on enhanced group dynamics.

o Senior management proficiency supported by a significant track record in the international automotive industry.

o Interface proficiency with upper management, key decision makers as well as Japanese and European representatives.

o Hands-on experience in automotive technical service, diagnostics, and repair.

o Demonstrated expertise in such areas as order processing, quality control, quality assurance, and customer relations.

o Comprehensive troubleshooting and problem solving skills with hands-on experience in repair, electrical and electronic diagnosis particularly with test technology pertinent to international applications.

o Knowledgeable of sales and service operations, interdepartmental coordination expertise for increased operational efficiency and account revenue.

o Excellent organizational skills include the ability to handle a variety of challenging assignments simultaneously.

o Extensive warranty claims analysis background including

familiarization with OSHA safety regulations and hazardous waste management.

o Personnel skills include hiring, training, staff development and performance evaluations as well as scheduling and master

Dr. Lawrence Peterson

BANKING
Bank Senior Manager

Over 16 years' experience in management supported by a track record for significantly improving operational efficiency in a bank lending environment.

Comprehensive operational expertise includes Profit and Loss accountability, budgeting, forecasting, projecting and expense control to maximize profitability.

Strong finance and analytical background including excellent investment skills relative to bank portfolios, including serving on the bank Asset Liability Committee.

Familiar with all areas of bank operations for a $390 million in assets bank, including international, credit cards, trust and personal money orders operations, and payroll processing.

Knowledge of checking account item processing, from bank of deposit to check writers bank including strong cash management abilities relative to check clearing to maximize availability of funds and reduce costs.

Demonstrated interface proficiency with management, key decision makers and affiliated personnel to further organizational policies and objectives.

Seasoned interpersonal communication skills in addition to strategic policy initiation for enhanced cooperation and rapport in meeting forecasted goals.

Capable of hiring, evaluating, training and motivating staff personnel for improved performance, productivity and organizational commitment.

Sound analytical decision making abilities supported by scheduling, master scheduling, manpower planning and manpower utilization to maximize capital and human resources.

Facilitate manpower utilization through training, cross training and development.

Mortgage Banker

o Several years progressive experience in mortgage banking backed by significant business development proficiency.

o Comprehensive business start-up background includes staff development and heavy interface with loan sources.

o Extensive account troubleshooting and problem solving skills regarding loan package analysis and underwriting requirements for expedient processing.

o Market data skills and demographic proficiency to initiate promotional strategies necessary for improving market penetration.

o Have performed client needs assessments in conjunction with understanding of consumer behavior for increased revenue.

o Experience servicing the challenging needs of multiple branches as well as large accounts volume simultaneously.

o Capable of providing effective leadership in pressure oriented environments to meet scheduled deadlines.

o Familiar with a variety of loan processing specializations in such areas as automotive financing and construction lending.

o Interface with clients, attorneys, lending and real estate personnel for improved account revenue.

o Outstanding oral and written communication skills supported by interpersonal competence for enhanced rapport and cooperation with clients and co-workers.

o Staff training and development abilities includes policy initiation and performance evaluations for improved performance, productivity and commitment.

Loan Officer

Commercial Loan Officer seeks increased responsibility in a challenging financial environment where experience can be applied to the efficient satisfaction of finance objectives.

Summary of Qualifications

o Over 16 years' experience in finance operations backed by expertise in commercial lending which includes construction loans and experience dealing with multi-million dollar transactions.

o Interface proficiency with brokers, contractors and the general public to increase real estate production.

o Comprehensive ability to increase sales through business development expertise.

o Experience with personal and auto loan packages complemented with extensive troubleshooting and problem solving skills.

o Demonstrated budgeting and forecasting proficiency with business turnaround experience resulting in increased profit and account revenue.

o Strong credit investigation and collections background supported by a working knowledge of small claims and bankruptcies.

o Seasoned negotiation skills include interface with management and customers for enhanced cooperation and rapport.

o Well-developed oral and written communication skills are supported by stand-up presentation capability.

BUSINESS SPECIALIST
Purchasing

Business specialist seeks increased responsibility as a Purchasing Agent where background and experience can be applied to the efficient satisfaction of organizational objectives.

Summary of Qualifications

o Over 16 years' experience in business operations backed by finance, budgeting and forecasting proficiency.

o Contract administration proficiency includes excellent negotiation and comparative price analysis abilities to obtain competitive bids and quotes.

o Able to effectively interface with vendors and sales representatives to secure necessary equipment and supplies.

o Analytical decision making abilities backed by extensive troubleshooting and problem solving for enhanced organizational efficiency.

o Strong supervisory skills supported by scheduling and manpower planning expertise for maximum utilization of human resources.

o Demonstrated ability to increase profits with a substantial cut in spending through inventory and cost control expertise.

o Possess an understanding of capital justifications and return on investment schedules.

o Solid credit investigation and collections background supported by a working knowledge of small claims and bankruptcies.

o Insight into commercial operations in a variety of settings.

o Personnel competence includes hiring, training, development, performance appraisals, and staff motivation.

o Outstanding oral and written communication skills.

BROKERING
Broker

Several years' progressive experience in management supported by extensive sales and marketing proficiency for enhanced account revenue.

Comprehensive operational competence includes Profit and Loss accountability, budgeting, forecasting, projecting in conjunction with an understanding of economic trend indicators.

Extensive account troubleshooting and problem solving skills pertinent to both tangible and intangible products and services to generate sales.

Demonstrated demographic expertise encompasses new territory development, trade show presentations, direct mail advertising and stand-up presentations to large companies and key decision makers.

Sound analytical decision making is supported by specialized knowledge of policies associated with Life, Property and Casualty, Auto, Disability, Buy and Sell Agreements.

Seasoned supervision skills include recruitment, scheduling and training of account representatives to generate new accounts as well as service existing transactions.

Consistently able to promote the most marketable elements of products and services through effective client needs assessments and product knowledge.

CRIMINAL JUSTICE
Criminal Justice

Over 10 years' experience in Law Enforcement.

Demonstrated competence in forensic investigation including expertise as a fingerprint and photography expert.

New technology implementation relative to lasers, cameras, and video evidence.

Prioritizing proficiency relative to case load management and complemented by extensive administrative skills relative to filing, recording and documentation.

Facilitate detectives with crime analysis as well as serve as an expert authority relative to "rules of evidence.

Possess outstanding public relations abilities with stand-up presentation capability pertinent to police policies and procedures.

Numerous contacts with other police agencies including interface proficiency with L.A. and S.B. crime labs.

Exposure to data processing and statistical analysis.

Staff training and development abilities.

Expertise in Sexual Child Abuse and Domestic Violence with the ability to acquire successful courtroom testimony.

Social Agency assistance in the placement of Abused, Incorrigible and Negligence victims.

Experience with community service drug programs with participation in undercover surveillance of narcotics transactions.

Demonstrated investigation ability with a comprehensive knowledge of P.C.P. Heroin and Cocaine as well as homicide investigations and suspect apprehensions.

COMMUNITY RESOURCES
Community Resources

Several years' responsible experience in community program activities.

Expertise in coordinating excursions, parties, special events and guest speakers.

Extensive troubleshooting and problem solving skills, to include disciplinary problem resolution.

Proficient in public speaking relative to on-going programs as well as staff presentations.

Demonstrated leadership abilities for enhanced organizational efficiency.

Experienced in annual budget preparation including weekly, monthly and yearly reports.

Heavy scheduling experience relative to staff agendas and special events.

Supervision of instructional specialists and evaluators including policy and procedure initiation for enhanced operational efficiency.

Comprehensive computer exposure - IBM, CRT for enhanced data processing.

Outstanding oral and written communication skills complemented by interpersonal skills for enhanced rapport and public relations.

Dr. Lawrence Peterson

Fire Battalion Chief

Battalion Chief seeks increased responsibility as a Division Chief where extensive background and experience can be applied to the efficient satisfaction of divisional objectives.

Summary of Qualifications

o Over 25 years' experience in Fire Service supported by seven years as a Battalion Chief.

o Extensive troubleshooting and problem solving skills to rapidly diagnose and remedy operational and organizational dysfunctions.

o Administrative skills include initiation and implementation abilities for division budgeting and establishing cost estimates for capital projects, outlay items and assets.

o Proficient in recruiting, interviewing, evaluating, and selecting new applicants is backed by designing and administering oral, written, and physical agility tests.

o Demonstrated interface proficiency with management, key decision makers and affiliated personnel to further organizational policies and objectives.

o Sound analytical decision making abilities applicable to scheduling, master scheduling, manpower planning and manpower utilization to maximize capital and human resources.

o Seasoned interpersonal communication skills involve stand-up presentation proficiency for enhanced cooperation and rapport in meeting forecasted goals.

o Consistently able to function effectively in pressure situations to meet scheduled deadlines as well as to expediently handle crisis and emergency situations.

o Capable of hiring, evaluating, training and motivating staff personnel for enhanced performance, productivity and organizational commitment.

Firefighter

Over 7 years' experience in firefighting while providing critical leadership from a technical and personnel perspective for improved readiness and response to emergencies.

Comprehensive troubleshooting and problem solving skills range in application from equipment inspections to hazardous materials.

Demonstrated ability to organize and direct the activities of affiliated fire personnel to expedite emergency operations while preserving evidence.

Sound analytical decision making abilities with regard to critical inspections and fire prevention recommendations in compliance with state and federal regulations.

Seasoned ability to identify training needs and create specialized curriculum materials to facilitate the achievement of necessary educational initiatives.

Consistently able to coordinate effective maintenance and preventative maintenance in conjunction with fire suppression equipment, facilities, trucks and associated equipment.

Capable of interfacing effectively with citizens and co-workers of diverse cultural backgrounds to generate enhanced rapport and cooperation.

Familiar with prevailing rules and regulations regarding fire prevention and suppression is supported by effective fact finding and evidence gathering proficiency.

Well-developed oral and written communication skills complemented by excellent documentation competence.

Firefighter-Paramedic

Fire Fighter - Paramedic seeks increased responsibility in a challenging municipal environment where background can be efficiently applied to the satisfaction of health and safety objectives.

Summary of Qualifications

o Comprehensive paramedic experience is supported by demonstrated life support, firefighting and medical proficiencies.

o Analytical skills allow for rapid assessment of emergencies pertinent to firefighting, medical aid, fire prevention inspection, and citizen assistance.

o Demonstrated leadership abilities to expedite organizational efficiency and team cooperation with co-workers and community representatives.

o Interpersonal communication expertise includes training abilities with firefighters and Emergency Medical Technicians.

o Proficient in public relations and community program activities relative to CPR and overall community relations.

o Computer exposure with Macintosh and IBM equipment, including LOTUS 1-2-3, Word and DBase software for enhanced data processing.

o Seasoned ability to identify training needs and create specialized curriculum materials to facilitate the achievement of necessary educational initiatives.

o Outstanding oral and written communication skills supported by Spanish facility.

o Able to adapt quickly to new organizational settings.

Fire Science-Instructor

Over 16 years' experience as an Emergency Fire Fighter supported by 12 years as a Fire Science Instructor, and 7 years as an Acting Captain.

Proficient in effectively coordinating the educational planning of the Fire Technology Program, as well as providing continuous evaluation to increase efficiency and productivity.

Administrative skills include division budgeting, enrollment and staff projecting, as well as class schedule preparation proficiency.

Expertise creating and administering a Recruitment Information Program resulting in substantial increases in new applicants.

Proficient in interviewing, evaluating, and selecting new applicants, including administering oral, written, and physical agility tests.

Personnel skills include performing orientation of new staff members for Fire Academies and State Marshall classes.

Extensive troubleshooting and problem solving abilities.

Able to effectively interface with people from varied cultural backgrounds.

Qualified under California State Plan for Vocational Education, as well as qualified for a California Community College Supervisory Credential.

Dr. Lawrence Peterson

Parks and Recreation

Over 14 years' experience in landscape design and maintenance backed by extensive coordination with developers, contractors, architects and City officials.

Comprehensive supervisory skills pertinent to the completion of field landscape checks, critiques, landscape plans and plan checks.

Extensive troubleshooting and problem solving skills includes park design, trees, plants, ground covers, plant suitability and irrigation.

Demonstrated ability to provide for the establishment and upkeep of appropriate record keeping to track projects during all phases.

Sound investigation skills to insure that proposed landscape installations conform to approved project plans and City standards.

Participate with City project review groups to provide input regarding landscape development projects.

Consistently able to oversee landscape design and development with particular attention to attractiveness and functionality.

Capable of providing contracts with continuity with the City master landscape design.

Familiar with all aspects of commercial, industrial and residential landscape applications.

Routinely issue necessary landscape maintenance performance bonds to assure conformance to City requirements.

Police Officer

Over 22 years in law enforcement backed by several years of

responsible supervisory experience.

Comprehensive knowledge of the principles, practices, and procedures of police work.

Extensive exposure to Penal, Civil, Vehicle, Health & Safety, Welfare & Institutions, Business & Professions, and Education Codes.

Troubleshooting and problem solving skills supported by the ability to plan, direct, and coordinate field and station activities.

Demonstrated capacity to function effectively in high pressure situations.
Preliminary and on-going crime scene investigation skills.

Interpersonal skills for enhanced rapport and cooperation. Seasoned experience in crime report analysis, correction, record keeping, and manpower utilization.

Experience handling K-9 units including budgeting, and recommendations for enhanced proficiency.

Assisted in developing a department aviation program.

Received distinguished service award for leadership in a major homicide investigation.

Recruitment, training and development abilities, in addition to employee evaluations.

Member of California Organization of Police Officers and Sheriffs.

Public Affairs

Over 20 years' experience in public affairs requiring the co-ordination of conventions, meetings, athletic and entertainment events.

Comprehensive ability to function as an effective liaison to media representatives to foster a positive public image.

Extensive troubleshooting and problem solving skills for effective coordination of support services and personnel.

Demonstrated contract administration and budget development are backed by seasoned marketing, sales, and fund-raising activities.

Consistently able to orchestrate and publicize special community events for a large number of people.

Capable of interfacing with such City personnel as the Mayor, City Council, City Manager and other staff persons to develop strategies for addressing particular issues.

Familiar with conducting media relations to explain operations, programs and issues, including writing articles and letters.

Exceptional interpersonal relations abilities for enhanced rapport and cooperation with media personnel, community representatives and co-workers.

Knowledge of public relations techniques and practices, including journalism ethics, public administration principles, public speaking and local laws and codes.

Can communicate both orally and in writing in addition to performing research and presenting pertinent data on findings.

Staff training and development abilities include developing an effective working relationship with others.

Public Works Inspection

Public Works Inspector seeks increased responsibility in a challenging environment where background can be efficiently applied to the satisfaction of organizational objectives.

Summary of Qualifications

o Public Works experience backed by a track record for improving operational efficiency.

o Comprehensive inspection skills pertinent to such projects as sewer and storm drains, sidewalks, roads and highways.

o Extensive troubleshooting and problem solving skills for the rapid diagnosis and remedy of on-site inspections per specification and standards prior to releasing for delivery.

o Demonstrated ability to perform manpower planning and project scheduling for a maximum return on human and fiscal resources.

o Pipeline construction experience includes both pressure and gravity configurations.

o Soil compaction, asphalt, concrete, and reinforced concrete expertise for application to a variety of project requirements.

o Consistently able to supervise General Contractors as well as all work according to prevailing specifications and standards.

o Capable of making strategic recommendations to improve operational performance as well as material usage.

o In addition to the ability to perform equipment designs, can provide field support for equipment and machinery repairs.

o Interface with vendors regarding plant and product inspections.

o Strong oral and written communication skills backed by a facility with Spanish.

o Staff training and development abilities.

Wastewater Specialist

Wastewater specialist seeks increased responsibility in a challenging environment where background and experience can be applied to the efficient satisfaction of organizational objectives.

Summary of Qualifications

o Experience with industrial and commercial waste water management is backed by strong investigation abilities.

o Demonstrated expertise in waste water analysis pertinent to carbon species and other ion concentrations utilizing the HACH chemical analysis kit.

o Extensive troubleshooting and problem solving skills, from preparing sampling equipment and taking samples, to interpreting laboratory procedures and performing follow-ups.

o Familiar with microbiology analysis including culturing experience to establish organism presence encompassing grid count to identify limits.

o Versed with titrimetric analysis to establish chemical concentrations.

o Can identify different types of parasites, from viruses to helminthes as well as versed with titrimetric analysis to establish chemical concentrations.

o Routinely conduct on-site pre-treatment equipment installations and inspections as well as follow-ups on spills and discharge source causation.

o Conduct waste water sampling and flow measurement analyses in addition to experience inspecting backflow devices and cross connections for compliance.

o Experienced in the usage of various lab equipment such as the spectrophotometer, including Radio Isotope applications, as well as laboratory procedures utilizing appropriate safety standards.

o Analytical decision making abilities supported by an orientation to detail with an emphasis on accuracy and precision.

Water Works

o Over 8 years' experience in water treatment operations.
o Comprehensive analysis and testing expertise relative to waste water.
o Extensive troubleshooting and problem solving skills.
o Demonstrated ability to maintain EPA and state regulations.
o Sound maintenance and repair skills relative to pumps, motors, and valves.
o Backflow testing proficiency, including addressing industrial cross connection concerns.
o Consistently perform water distribution activities to satisfy customer requirements.
o Capable of supervising technicians as well as construction personnel.
o Biological samplings, documentation, and follow-up.
o Interface with engineers, state officials and EPA representatives, as well as with customers.
o Facilitate organizational efficiency through strong scheduling skills and supervisory abilities.

COMMUNICATIONS
Communications Specialist

Experience with audio-visual equipment, including video tape production using a porta-pack.

Ability to compose newsletters, including paste-up, layout and offset printing.

Proficiency with brochures, press releases and related materials for publication or broadcast applications.

Extensive troubleshooting and problem solving skills.

Computer competence with all Windows programs including Word, Lotus 1-2-3 & DBase III.

Sound writing and editing skills - maintained computer mailing list as well as performed managing editor and contributing writer functions.

Produced an occupational therapy tape subsequently used by Riverside Community Hospital.

Am familiar with a variety of office related equipment, from folding machines to stencil makers.

Possess insight into accounting functions and procedures. Familiar with a variety of electronic products as well as applications.

Audio-Visual Specialist

Experience with audio-visual equipment, including video tape production using a porta-pack.

Ability to compose newsletters, including paste-up, layout and offset printing.

Proficiency with brochures, press releases and related materials for publication or broadcast applications.

Extensive troubleshooting and problem solving skills.

Computer competence with Word, Lotus 1-2-3 & DBase III.

Sound writing and editing skills - maintained computer mailing list as well as performed managing editor and contributing writer functions.

Produced an occupational therapy tape subsequently used by Riverside Community Hospital.

Am familiar with a variety of office related equipment, from folding machines to stencil makers.

Possess insight into accounting functions and procedures.

Familiar with a variety of electronic products as well as applications.

Outstanding oral and written communication skills.

Able to adapt quickly to new organizational settings.

Communications Technician

Over seven year's progressive experience with independent interconnect systems with a track record for successfully implementing custom configurations.

Comprehensive contracting and subcontracting expertise to expedite project objectives for such organizations as Kraft Foods, Drug Emporium, Carpeteria, and the Union Land Title Company.

Extensive system troubleshooting and problem solving skills with such equipment as the Zenith Computer and the Panasonic Dummy Terminal to diagnose and optimize system performance and integrity.

Demonstrated project installation scheduling as well as prewiring and set-ups in addition to cable engineering for new and existing facilities.

Sound electrical blueprint and wiring schematic reading proficiency supported by equipment selections and custom programming endeavors.

Seasoned profit and loss accountability backed by budgeting, forecasting and projecting proficiency.

Consistently able to perform accurate needs assessments and bid proposals, including RFP's for state and federal applications.

Capable of performing efficient least cost routing and automatic route selection activities with an emphasis on quality.

Communication and Navigation Specialist

Communication and Navigation specialist seeks increased responsibility in a challenging environment where background can be efficiently applied to the satisfaction of technical objectives.

Summary of Qualifications

o Extensive troubleshooting and problem solving skills pertinent to sophisticated configurations for enhanced system integrity, maintenance and performance.

o Demonstrated ability to perform inspection, maintenance and repair to the component level utilizing extensive understanding of aircraft communication-navigation technology as well as the latest maintenance directives.

o Experience consolidating work centers in conjunction with inspecting, servicing and ensuring correct documentation of calibration for over 250 pieces of test equipment.

o Consistently able to provide for leadership of other technicians through strategic interpersonal relations and technical competence.

o Cash awards for cost efficiency recommendations pertinent to time and documentation manuals along with authoring hazard reports.

o Strong fiscal competence includes budgeting and forecasting, as well as inventory control and manpower planning.

o Facilitate enhanced quality assurance through strong diagnostic and inspection proficiency in pressure situations to meet scheduled deadlines.

o Outstanding oral and written communication skills are backed by precise documentation and reporting.

o Staff training and development abilities in addition to performance evaluations for improved performance, productivity and accuracy.

Communications Technician

Communications Technician seeks increased responsibility in a challenging environment where background and experience can be applied to the efficient satisfaction of organizational objectives.

Summary of Qualifications

o Several years responsible experience in data communications backed by extensive troubleshooting and problem solving skills.

o Experienced as a Cryptographic Machine Operator and as an Automatic Data Communications Operator.

o Comprehensive ability to conduct design and engineering tasks relative to fiber-optic cable installations, as well as make cost estimating recommendations in support of telecommunications objectives.

o Skilled in analyzing complex voice and data communication systems and networking to plan for system upgrades.

o Working knowledge of principles of cable plant engineering including nomenclature, industry standards, methods, and sources of information.

o Excellent analytical research skills to evaluate telecommunications product effectiveness.

o Interpret technical documents relative to communication interface devices on computerized telecommunication systems.

o Experience in operation, maintenance, and repair of fixed station communications equipment and systems relative to Automated Data Systems and Cryptographic Equipment.

o DoD security clearance with EBI.

o Outstanding oral and written communication skills.

o Staff training and development abilities.

Public Affairs

Progressive Public Affairs experience with a track record for developing and implementing major Public Information Systems.

Comprehensive ability to function as an effective liaison to media representatives to foster a positive public image.

Extensive troubleshooting and problem solving skills pertinent to handling media inquiries and press releases for special circumstances.

Demonstrated ability to prepare and review press releases, articles, and newsletters as well as other internal and external communication.

Knowledge of the principles and practices of effective public relations, including journalism, public relations and management.

Interface with city and media representatives to gather and verify news as well as prepare stories from a particular slant.

Graphic arts proficiency pertinent to flyers, brochures, and promotional materials, including photography.

Exceptional interpersonal abilities for enhanced rapport and cooperation with media personnel, community representatives and coworkers.

Outstanding oral and written communication skills backed by staff training and development abilities as well as fluency in Italian and stand-up presentation capabilities.

Public Information Specialist

Several years' responsible experience in Public Affairs with a track record for developing and implementing a major Public Information Program.

Comprehensive ability to function as an effective liaison to media representatives to foster a positive public image.

Extensive troubleshooting and problem solving skills pertinent to handling media inquiries and press releases for such special circumstances as disasters.

Demonstrated ability to prepare and review press releases, articles and newsletters as well as other internal and external communication.

Sound audio-visual competence in conjunction with stand-up presentations to community representatives.

Experience providing current affairs information, preparing speeches and presenting multi-media presentations.

Consistently able to orchestrate and publicize special community events for a large number of people.

Knowledge of the principles and practices of effective public relations, including journalism, public administration and management.

Familiar with all aspects of newswriting, news media sources and resources with the ability to research and prepare concise reports, newsletters and multi-media releases.

Interface with city and media representatives to gather and verify news as well as prepare stories from a particular slant.

Computer competent with Word, Bankstreet Writer, Photoshop, Easy Write, Lotus 1-2-3 and Quark Express.

Outstanding oral and written communication skills backed

by fluency in English, German, and French with proficiency in Italian.

COMPUTERS
Computer Applications

Computer Applications Specialist seeks increased responsibility in a challenging environment where background can be efficiently applied to the satisfaction of system objectives.

Summary of Qualifications

o Over 20 years responsible experience with computers in such capacities as Senior Engineer, Quality Assurance Supervisor, Senior Programmer, and Systems Analyst.

o Achievements include designing diagnostic programs, RPG II Compiler, Application Test Programs and test tools for Quality Assurance software certification.

o Comprehensive understanding of computer technology, software development, software quality assurance and technical support for enhanced system integrity and customer satisfaction.

o Extensive troubleshooting and problem solving skills to diagnose and remedy system dysfunctions for a variety of custom business applications, including Optical Character Readers.

o Demonstrated ability to effectively develop test plans and procedures in addition to fostering policies and procedures for improved quality and operational efficiency.

o Analytical decision making abilities include monitoring development activity as well as performing audits to maintain strict Quality Assurance standards and practices.

o Seasoned client interpersonal communication skills as well as the ability to deal with individuals from diverse cultural backgrounds.

o Well-developed oral and written communication skills in

addition to staff training and development abilities.

Hardware
IBM, WYSE, Hyundai, VAX 750, Epson, Texas Instrument, Cannon, and Xerox Printers...

Software
Windows, MS-DOS, UNIX, dBASE, Assembly Language.

Languages
CADOL, Perl, PASCAL, RPG, BASIC, "C", Java, Python and AJAX.

Computer Operations

Responsible experience in business and computer operations backed by a track record for facilitating operational efficiency.

Comprehensive troubleshooting and problem solving skills pertinent to computer system activities as well as customer service endeavors.

Demonstrated analytical decision making abilities backed by an attention to detail and strong organizational skills.

Sound math proficiency includes calculus and accounting competency.

Seasoned computer literacy includes JCL language proficiency as well as Cobol familiarity.

Consistently able to monitor central processing units and minicomputer operations.

Capable of executing jobs according to priority, availability, and sequential processing requirements.

Operate magnetic tape units, high speed printers and can maintain records of routine and abnormal processing terminations and job completions.

Interface with various inter-departmental personnel in addition to such other agencies as the Sheriff's Department and local hospitals for enhanced system integrity.

Computer Customer Service

Customer service problem solving skills in addition to inter-personal competence for enhanced rapport and cooperation with clients and co-workers.

Extensive troubleshooting and problem solving skills from board to component level in addition to networking to set up complete computer systems for local companies.

Microcomputer hardware repairs to the component level, as well as peripheral installation and repair of disk drives, keyboards, video displays, hard disks and printers.

Experienced with MS DOS, Word, Dbase III Plus, LOTUS 1-2-3 and various diagnostic and virus protection programs.

Capable of reading electronic schematics and blue prints in addition to familiarity with such equipment as VOM, DMM, Oscilloscope, logic probes and logic analyzers.

Well-developed oral and written communication skills supported by Spanish facility.

CNC
CNC Programming

Extensive experience in programming machines for efficient production machining.

Over 12 years in jig and fixture building, template and plaster/pattern making, and precision development mechanics.

Demonstrated competency in the use of such precision measuring instruments as height gauges, indicators, transits and levels.

Very competent in the use of shop math, as well as proficiency in reading and interpreting blueprints.

Strong layout, fabrication, and optical instrument ability relative to major A.J.'s and sub-assembly fixtures.

Working knowledge and hands-on experience with all types of approved materials: metals, wood, plastic, and composites.

Capable of working from engineering specifications to adhere to close tolerances - (.0002).

Experience in modification, overhaul, and repair of major aircraft components.

Work from M.L.O.'s and engineering data to manufacture various templates and form blocks to engineering drawings.

Produced one-dimensional drawings on decoat and mylar for flat pattern development.

Experienced with exotic materials - titanium, beryllium etc. Extensive troubleshooting and problem solving skills. Staff training and development abilities.

CAD

Progressive experience in mechanical design engineering for

effective project development.

Comprehensive design and redesign experience, from concept through production.

Extensive troubleshooting and problem solving skills.

Demonstrated proficiency in proposal development.

Sound cost reduction through alternate designs and parts simplification.

Computer experience 2D, 3Dm CAD/CAM software and Solid-Works.

Proficient with ANSI Y 14.5 to satisfy geometric dimension objectives.

Familiar with PERT, CPM, and Gantt charting for scheduling.

Excellent understanding of machine shop practices, including tooling and fixtures.

Inspection and non-destructive testing expertise, including vibration tests and isolation tests.

Knowledge of casting relative to design applications.

Interface proficiency with vendors, electrical, machine shop, test equipment and the program office personnel.

COMPUTER APPLICATIONS
Computer Specialist

Computer Applications Specialist seeks increased responsibility in a challenging environment where background can be efficiently applied to the satisfaction of system objectives.

Summary of Qualifications

o Over 22 years responsible experience with computers in such capacities as Senior Engineer, Quality Assurance Supervisor, Senior Programmer, and Systems Analyst.

o Achievements include designing diagnostic programs, RPG II Compiler, Application Test Programs and test tools for Quality Assurance software certification.

o Comprehensive understanding of computer technology, software development, software quality assurance and technical support for enhanced system integrity and customer satisfaction.

o Extensive troubleshooting and problem solving skills to diagnose and remedy system dysfunctions for a variety of custom business applications, including Optical Character Readers.

o Demonstrated ability to effectively develop test plans and procedures in addition to fostering policies and procedures for improved quality and operational efficiency.

o Analytical decision making abilities include monitoring development activity as well as performing audits to maintain strict Quality Assurance standards and practices.

o Seasoned client interpersonal communication skills as well as the ability to deal with individuals from diverse cultural backgrounds.

o Well-developed oral and written communication skills in

addition to staff training and development abilities.

Hardware
IBM, WYSE, Hyundai, VAX 750, Epson, Texas Instrument, Epson, HP, and General Electric Printers

Software
MS-DOS, UNIX, DOS 3.3, dBASE, Assembly Language
Languages CADOL, PASCAL, Perl, AJAX, Java, RPG, BASIC, "C", SQL

Data Processing

Data Processing professional seeks increased responsibility in a challenging environment where technical background and training proficiency can be efficiently applied to the satisfaction of operational objectives.

Summary of Qualifications

o Over 10 years diversified experience in computer networking backed by supervisory proficiency and technical knowledge of data processing applications.

o Extensive troubleshooting and problem solving skills pertinent to operational computer systems for the rapid diagnosis and remedy of data dysfunctions.

o Proficient in analyzing data communication systems and networking to plan for system upgrades as well as to foster improved data efficiency.

o Seasoned interface skills with upper management, co-workers and customers for smooth transition and integration of new computer applications.

o Consistently able to coordinate large and multiple projects simultaneously to meet scheduled deadlines.

o Scheduling and manpower planning proficiency to maximize human and capital resources.

o Capable of providing technical support for managers and interdepartmental personnel for enhanced system integrity.

o Computer literate with IBM compatible equipment and software demonstrating expertise with PARADOX, Word, Norton Utility, LOTUS 1-2-3. QuickBooks, DOS and Quark.

o Outstanding oral and written communication skills with stand-up presentation capability.

o Extensive staff training and development abilities with particular emphasis on programming and computer applications.

Dr. Lawrence Peterson

MIS

MIS Specialist with Systems Engineering Support expertise seeks increased opportunity to maximize operational effectiveness.

Summary of Qualifications

o Experienced with structured programming concepts, data base constructs, and 10 programming languages ranging from FORTRAN, COBOL, Perls, AJAX, PASCAL, ADA and C.

o Combine a rare sense of practicality with extensive experience and technical knowledge in implementing configuration management and system engineering planning.

o Strong troubleshooting and problem solving competence in defining, recommending and improving data systems management.

o Success in managing groups of project engineers and computer systems analysts in support of complex communication programs.

o Experience performing configuration control planning on multi-billion dollar programs, including policy initiation for enhanced compliance.

o Adept at performing user needs assessments to design and implement computer systems for a variety of applications and operational areas.

o Extensive business analysis and reporting skills relative to feasibility, efficiency, and cost benefit of recommended systems.

o Comprehensive system troubleshooting and debugging expertise utilizing strong diagnostic skills to maximize system performance and enhance uptime.

o Technical methodologies, both theoretical and practical,

encompassing design, writing, and testing of underlying software.

o Analytical decision making abilities for increased organizational efficiency backed by manpower planning and scheduling competence for the maximum utilization of human resources.

Network Services

Manager of Network Services seeks increased responsibility in a challenging environment where background can be efficiently applied to the satisfaction of operational objectives.

Summary of Qualifications

o Over 16 years diversified experience in telecommunications backed by technical knowledge of specialized equipment used for voice, data and alarm applications.

o Comprehensive understanding of all types of conditioning and signaling as outlined in the tariffs on file with the California PUC and FCC.

o Extensive troubleshooting and problem solving skills of transmission systems for the rapid diagnosis and remedy of data dysfunctions.

o Demonstrated ability to utilize state-of-art test equipment in addition to providing feedback regarding findings, potential down and restoration time.

o Proficient in analyzing complex voice and data communication systems and networking to plan for system upgrades.

o Seasoned interface skills with Design Analysis and Interconnect Designers for smooth transition and operational efficiency.

o Consistently able to coordinate large and multiple projects simultaneously to meet scheduled deadlines.

o Scheduling and manpower planning proficiency to maximize human and capital resources.

o Capable of providing technical support for Controller Testers, outside field, installation, maintenance and affiliated personnel for enhanced system integrity.

o Outstanding oral and written communication skills.

MIS Manager

Several years' responsible experience in programming and system analysis backed by software modification and data conversion expertise.

Administrative competence includes budgeting, forecasting and projecting departmental needs as well as policies and procedures for improved system integrity and performance.

Demonstrated accounting exposure includes receivables, payables, collections, General Ledger, fixed assets, purchasing, MRP, job costing, capital reporting and wholesale distribution.

Extensive troubleshooting and problem solving skills pertinent to hardware, peripherals and software configurations.

Additional expertise in construction scheduling, sales, customer service, contract administration and property management.

Management skills include master scheduling, manpower planning and direct supervision of department personnel to accomplish accounting objectives.

Interface with virtually all organizational personnel, from office support through upper management to expedite data processing endeavors.

Facilitated the development and installation of electronic data capture system for credit cards utilized in Ramada Inns throughout the country.

Hardware
IBM Mainframes: ZEC12, Cloud, and older 308X, 33XX, 43XX, AS400, S38; ATT 3B2; Tandem Non-Stop; and such PC systems as XT, AT, 386 PS/2.

Software

McCormack and Dodge Millennium General Ledger, MSA Human Resource Management System, McCormack and Dodge Capital Projects Analysis and Accounting System, McCormick and Dodge Fixed Assets, American Software Institute Purchasing and Customer Order Entry, and the McCosker Construction Software Package.

Languages
C, Java, Perl, AJAX, Mark IV, COBOL, Basic, JCL, UNIX, OS/MVS, Guardian, and Pathway.

Network Manager

Several years' experience in computer operations backed by equipment and software selection to maximize data processing objectives.

Comprehensive troubleshooting and problem solving skills pertinent to hardware and peripherals, software, and custom applications in a variety of environments for improved uptime and system optimization.

Diversified program applications include automated distribution, inventory control, general ledger, billing, receivables, payables, payroll and rate quotes.

Sound analytical decision making competence with the added ability to handle multiple projects simultaneously.

Sound staff training and development proficiency to maximize human and capital resources as well as promote enhanced data processing efficiency.

Strong writing skills include user training manuals relative to hardware and operation parameters for enhanced system performance and integrity
.

Capable of performing needs assessments relative to software and hardware requirements in addition to budgeting and estimating department requirements.

Maintain expertise with various software packages sustained by new application development, production support and technical writing proficiency.

Can organize as well as facilitate computer networking endeavors through understanding of system capabilities as well as experience in custom hardware and software packages.

Hardware
TANDEM VLX, IBM 3090, IBM 3279, IBM 3292 E/A, DEC

10, NORTHSTAR, and IBM PC's and compatibles in various configurations.

Software
GUARDIAN 90, TACL, PATHWAY, SPOOLCOM, TAPECOM, PER-USE, IBM TSO, ISIM, FOCUS, PC DOS, NOVELL NETWARE, dBASE IV, PLUS, BASIC, FOCUS, COBOL, PCL, C, Lotus 1-2-3, Word, Quark and many more.

o Extensive programming experience.
o UNIX, VMS, KEX, PROFS, VM/CMS, GEMS, LOTUS 1-2-3.
o Have knowledge of construction of digital interface circuits
o Oral and written fluency in Cantonese and Mandarin.
o Adapt quickly to new organizational settings.

Selected Coursework

Software Engineering, Microprocessors, Software Evaluation, Computer Architecture, Data Base Systems, Logical System Design, Numerical Analysis, Electrical Circuits and Systems, Linear Programming, Data Structure Techniques, Systems Programming, Algorithm Design and Analysis, FORTRAN Programming, Compiler Design, PASCAL Programming, Operating System, Programming Languages, Discrete Mathematical Assembly Language Structures for Computer, Programming and Science Computer Organization Computer Languages FORTRAN, PASCAL, Perl, AJAX, Assembly, ABDA, LISP, BASIC, SIMSCRIPT, C Computer Systems, VAX, HP 9000, INTEL Z, Macintosh.

Programmer - Analyst

Knowledge of several computer languages including Fortran, Perl, AJAX, Java, Cobol, Model 204, and JCL.

Proficient with Word, Data Base V, Quark, Photoshop, and QuickBooks.

Troubleshooting and problem solving skills to maximize programming objectives.

Exposure to VAX, IBM Mainframe, Macintosh, Apple II, and Digital Rainbow 5000, in addition to Peripheral hardware.

Familiar with normalizing, entity charts, and conceptual diagrams to develop relational data bases.

Background in budgeting, forecasting, reporting, scheduling and manpower planning utilizing Gantt, CPM, and PERT charts.

Good oral and written communication skills - have delivered briefings to Vice Presidents, Project Managers as well as functional management.

Capable of designing systems using structure development methodology.

Familiar with maintenance and enhancements along with inventory, finance, and job order status development.

Served as Acting Project Manager on a $450,000 project involving the conversion from an old Cobol language to a relational data base system utilizing the Model 204 language.

Software Engineer

Lead engineer with project management experience.

Comprehensive programming expertise, Basic, Pascal, C, Perl, AJAX, FORTRAN, Python, Java and VB Net.

Extensive troubleshooting and problem solving skills to maintain system integrity
.

Demonstrated ability to design and create systems using structure development methodology.

Sound interface proficiency with all levels of project management and user personnel.

Seasoned technical supervision and evaluation of sub system performance.

Budgeting and estimating abilities.

Capable of working with MIL-STD 2167, as well as with rules and documents that go along with MIL-SPECs.

Developed, sold and installed an application system to Saudi Arabia Airlines.

Have written OS drivers and am familiar with RTE and RSX operating system internals.

Experience with real-time and applications programming.

Networks background, including 1553B BUS, Q-BUS, UNIBUS.

Systems Administrator for Hewlett Packard products.

Government Clearance: Active DoD Top Secret (TS) with Special Background Investigation (SBI/SI).

CONSTRUCTION
Construction Manager

Over 15 year's progressive experience in construction backed by such commercial applications as high-rise masonry.

Comprehensive understanding of California construction laws and regulations are backed by a General Contractor's License in Montana and a Masonry Contractors License in both Califoria and Montana.

Extensive project troubleshooting and problem solving skills; have supervised masonry projects in excess of $2 million.

Expertise with such materials as dimensional stone, brick-block, GFRC panels, and precast concrete panels.

Projects include hospitals, shopping centers, water treatment plants, power plants, schools and high-rise buildings.

Demonstrated ability to perform budgeting, forecasting and projecting, in addition to manpower planning for a maximum return on human resources.

Sound organizational and prioritization skills for enhanced project efficiency and control.

Seasoned personnel skills include hiring, evaluating and promoting individuals to increased levels of responsibility.

Interface with architects, contractors, subcontractors, vendors and inspection personnel to expedite project objectives.

Facilitate enhanced performance and productivity through policy and procedure recommendations.

Outstanding oral and written communication skills backed by staff training and development abilities.

Construction Communications Coordinator

Communications Consulting Coordinator seeks increased responsibility in a challenging construction environment where background can be efficiently applied to the satisfaction of technical objectives.

Summary of Qualifications

o Over 30 years responsible experience in communications backed by project management expertise for large housing tracts, commercial and industrial settings.

o Comprehensive technical skills includes planning, engineering and construction pertinent to such utility cable applications as T.V., Edison, Fiber Optic and Central Office telephone installation.

o Extensive project troubleshooting and problem solving skills include capital justifications, manpower planning and field audits.

o Demonstrated Profit and Loss accountability applicable to budgeting, forecasting and projecting as well as bidding and contract negotiation.

o Sound analytical decision making abilities are backed by knowledge of GO-95 requirements as well as local, county, state and federal regulations.

o Seasoned marketing competence includes project presentations to key decision makers, networking, referrals, direct mail and trade show development.

o Consistently able to function effectively in pressure environments to meet scheduled deadlines.

o Capable of interfacing with developers, architects, inspectors, and affiliated field personnel.

o Outstanding oral and written communication skills backed by staff training and development abilities.

Supervisor-Foreman

Construction Supervisor - Foreman seeks increased responsibility in a challenging environment where background can be efficiently applied to the satisfaction of project objectives.

Summary of Qualifications

o Responsible experience in construction backed by large project and multiple project exposure in conjunction with fast-tracking proficiency.

o Comprehensive project management abilities pertinent to residential, commercial and industrial assignments.

o Extensive project troubleshooting and problem solving skills include bidding, estimating, budgeting, contract administration and expense control to maximize capital and human resources.

o Have expedited purchasing, vendor negotiations, inventory control and distribution activities for optimal cost effectiveness within budgetary guidelines.

o Sound knowledge of building codes, local, state and federal regulations, permits and impact fees to promote project initiatives.

o Seasoned proficiency with sub-contractors, local planning councils, engineers and building officials to promote inspectional performance.

o Familiar with rough and finish carpentry, plumbing, electrical, glazing, masonry, form work, doors, steel stud framing, steel reinforced concrete and post tension concrete.

o Scheduling, manpower planning and manpower allocation expertise for the maximum utilization of equipment and material as well as to promote project efficiency.

o Field equipment maintenance, repair and operation regarding fork-lifts, flatbed trucks, skip loaders, and bobcats, as well as other associated equipment.

o Familiar with commercial and residential underground utilities in addition to paving, drainage systems and landscaping.

Construction Specialist

Construction specialist seeks increased responsibility in a challenging environment where background can be efficiently applied to the satisfaction of project objectives.

Summary of Qualifications

o Over 15 years progressive experience in construction backed by large project and multiple project exposure in conjunction with fast-tracking proficiency.

o Extensive project troubleshooting and problem solving expertise as well as experience with bidding, estimating and contract administration to maximize capital and human resources.

o Operational proficiency includes profit and loss accountability, budgeting, forecasting and projecting in addition to strategic expense control.

o Sound knowledge of building codes, local, state and federal regulations, permits and impact fees to foster project initiatives.

o Seasoned proficiency with sub-contractors, local planning councils, engineers and building officials to promote inspectional performance.

o Familiarity with all building trades is supported by custom home experience demonstrating attention to detail and quality assurance.

o Capable of performing vendor negotiations and purchasing in addition to inventory control for optimal cost effectiveness within budgetary guidelines.

o Scheduling, manpower planning and manpower allocation expertise for the maximum utilization of equipment and material as well as to enhance project efficiency.

o Familiar with residential underground utilities in addition to paving, drainage systems and landscaping.

o Personnel skills include hiring, evaluating, and training for increased performance, productivity, quality and safety.

Dr. Lawrence Peterson

COSMETOLOGY
Licensed Cosmetologist

License in cosmetology with an emphasis in theatrical make-up.
Comprehensive troubleshooting and problem solving skills.

Extensive knowledge of permanents, creative hair coloring, advanced hair cutting, weaving, and styling.

Hair styling ranges from conservative to heavy metal.

Have advanced training with various manufacturers products.

Demonstrated ability to perform makeovers, corrective make-up, day and night make-up.

Make-Up skills relative to stage applications and photo shoots such as New York West.

Can tie hair styles and make-up with specific clothing styles. Very fast and accurate - can wrap a permanent in 25 minutes.

Won award for most beautiful hair relative to beauty contest. Have experience with Pat Travers and Blue Oyster Cult bands.

Will be engaged in hair styling for Brittny Fox. Maintain currency with latest hair and make-up styles - trends.

COUNSELING
Counselor

Experience providing individual and group counseling to students, parents and school staff personnel.

Comprehensive ability to design and implement individualized programs to improve self-image as well as minimize behavioral problems with students.

Extensive therapeutic troubleshooting and problem solving skills, including intakes, assessments, diagnosis and treatment plans.

Demonstrated ability to promote a supportive and rewarding learning environment while assisting in the prevention and resolution of disabling educational, personal and social dysfunctions.

Consistently interact with educational staff personnel, administration and school psychologist to create individualized learning programs directed toward enhancing student achievement.

Capable of addressing the mental and emotional needs of students with moderate and severe histories of abuse and neglect.

Excellent documentation skills pertinent to case histories, incident reports and follow-ups.

Proficient with multi-disciplinary treatment team meetings as well as substance abuse program requirements.

Outstanding oral and written communication skills supported by staff training and development abilities to maximize capital and human resources.

Sound knowledge of social support services backed by practical experience dealing with a variety of cases - from child abuse to family dynamics.

Initiated and implemented drug counseling programs and life skills workshops for low income families.

Experience providing training and technical assistance for the Head Start Program at the University of Kansas.

Administration proficiency with budgets, projections, and scheduling, as well as grant and proposal writing.

Research experience encompassing litigation to support health claims made by individuals involving tobacco.

Extensive troubleshooting and problem solving skills supported by precise case management.

Experience dealing with Aids and Cerebral Palsy clients. Well-developed oral and written communication skills.

CREDIT
Credit and Collections

Over 11 years' experience in credit operations backed by sound management proficiency.

Comprehensive credit and collections expertise, including management reporting.

Extensive troubleshooting and problem solving skills.

Demonstrated ability to interface with all levels of management and peers, as well as credit and collection agencies,

Sound analytical skills for the rapid resolution of operational dysfunctions.

Seasoned decision making abilities, including authoring policies -wrote Southern California

Credit Policy for procedural uniformity.

Consistently able to maximize personnel resources through strategic hiring, training, performance appraisals and leadership skills.

Capable of performing timely diagnostic analysis with particular attention to prevention to enhance operational performance.

Familiar with such computer systems as CRT and IBM to expedite data processing objectives.

Can achieve targeted DSO objectives with out impacting sales growth.

Bad debt write off kept to within one-half of one percent of sales budget.

Created self-managing work unit to expedite accounts receivables.

Strong contacts with major banks, trade ground and trade associations.

Customer Service

Over 17 years' experience in warehouse distribution and customer service with additional management experience in Shipping and Receiving and Merchandising.

Expertise with surplus merchandise liquidations.

Staff training and troubleshooting seminars for group meetings.

Interface with Buyers, Merchandising Assistants, Store Managers and Customer Service Managers relative to expediting orders.

Experience with labor negotiations and grievance procedures.

Payroll budgeting for a department of 200 employees.

Scheduling and manpower planning for the Customer Service Dept.

Numerous cost cutting recommendations for increased efficiency.

Set department productivity standards for enhanced performance.

Inspection of incoming and outgoing goods for quality control.

Field liaison between selling units and distribution centers.

Export handling for Japan, Philippines and Pacific Islands.

Shipping expertise to Alaska, Hawaii and Western United States.

Random Order Maintenance System for enhanced inventory control.

Involved with new distribution center promotions.

Outstanding oral and written communication skills.

Adapt quickly to new organizational settings.

Extensive customer service problem solving skills.

EDUCATION
Elementary Teacher

Elementary teaching experience supported by a strong commitment to student achievement.

Comprehensive classroom management skills with expertise in assertive discipline and positive reinforcement.

Proficiency with clinical teaching methods to enhance student involvement.

Curriculum strengths include science, language arts integration, writing and social studies.
Athletically inclined to expedite physical education assignments with children.

Hands-on project development to facilitate student interest, i.e., archaeological dig and cultural communities.

Able to adapt teaching approach to varied student populations and learning curves.

Taught G.A.T.E. students in regular and summer school. Was a Master Teacher in summer school at Vina Danks Elementary School.

Heavily involved in in-service and staff development. Outstanding parent/staff interpersonal communication skills. Member of the Parent Teachers Association.

Learning Disability Specialist

Over 20 years in teaching backed by expertise in attending to the academic needs of students with learning disabilities.

Extensive experience administering and interpreting various types of psychometric and achievement test instruments.

Experienced in working with adults with learning problems.

Proficiency with planning and affecting diagnostic evaluations of students, as well as writing and implementing individual student education plans.

Schedule and facilitate student meetings to present assessment findings and to explain the education plans and implementation process.

Familiarity with state and federal laws regarding diagnosis of students with learning disabilities.
Curriculum development proficiency supported by a demonstrated ability to create specialized learning materials and utilization of compensatory methods.

Developed school staff and support personnel policies, procedures, and programs for special education departments.

Sound supervision skills relative to special education aides, consulting instructors, and counselors.

Ability to interface with various departments for enhanced team cooperation and rapport.

Capable of teaching students from a variety of cultural backgrounds, learning levels, and potentials.

Staff training and development abilities, including in-service programs.

Graduate coursework in counseling techniques and use of computers.

Dr. Lawrence Peterson

School Administrator

o Several years responsible experience in educational administration backed by teaching experience.

o Comprehensive knowledge and understanding of educational goals and objectives.

o Sound management proficiency for enhanced organizational development.

o Extensive troubleshooting and problem solving skills.

o Demonstrated budgeting and forecasting expertise.

o Successful experience complying with educational codes and testing requirements.

o Able to meet scheduled deadlines.

o Facilities planning, maintenance, and contract negotiation experience.

o Committee experience relative to the development of a district-wide math program.

o Experience as an Associated Student Council Advisor.

o Ability to communicate effectively with staff and parents.

o Effective disciplinarian for improved academic efficiency.

o Participate in various continuing education programs.

o Well developed oral and written communication skills.

o Staff training and development abilities.

o Able to adapt quickly to new organizational settings.

Teacher

Several years teaching and coaching experience in a variety of academic settings to accomplish scholastic and athletic objectives.

Comprehensive expertise teaching students from a variety of cultural backgrounds, learning levels, and potentials.

Extensive troubleshooting and problem solving skills through interface with parents, students and Administration.

Demonstrated ability to enhance classroom behavioral management for enhanced student achievement.

Proficient in dealing effectively with the emotional stages of adolescence in addition to high and low achieving students.

Seasoned organizational skills include curriculum development and multi-subject teaching competence.

Strong scheduling and development proficiency pertinent to school events, from Proms to specialized athletic events.

Capable of utilizing creative lesson plans to enhance student interest as well as performance.

Curricular experience includes Life Science, Remedial Math, Leadership, and Year Book utilizing computers.

Interface effectively with student body with regard to such sensitive issues as substance abuse.

Facilitate league initiatives through interaction with various sports officials as well as appropriate documentation for league and student eligibility.

TRAINING
Athletic Trainer

Comprehensive understanding of cardiovascular conditioning, durance training, and peak performance training.

Organizational skills relative to multi-sports events.

Effective planning proficiency for the triathlete novice.

Ability to teach beginning and advanced students.

Skill in working with all age groups in a variety of sports.

Make diet suggestions for enhanced performance.

Consistently emphasize prevention of sports injuries.

Successfully initiated and developed an aqua aerobics class.

Currently amateur rated triathlete.

Health equipment maintenance experience.

Coaching experience relative to form, style and endurance.

Nominated employee of the year.

Outstanding interpersonal communication skills.

Able to adapt quickly to new organizational settings.

Trainer

o Administrative competence in budgeting, forecasting and projecting is supported by extensive training experience in the health industry ranging from Hydrostatic Weighing and Anthropometric measurement to exercise prescriptions.

o Instructional background includes stress management, smoking abatement, nutrition, exercise and overall health which can be leveraged into other product and service presentations.

o Demonstrated proficiency with training needs assessments in conjunction with exercise prescriptions and the creation of specialized programs to meet individualized client needs.

o Comprehensive ability to promote the effective servicing of existing transactions, the opening of new territories and the launching of specialized products and services.

o Extensive troubleshooting and problem solving skills to rapidly identify and correct instructional dysfunctions for enhanced retention, repeat sales and referrals.

o Familiar with tangible and intangible account development to identify and capitalize on the most marketable attributes of a given product or service.

o High energy personality who can function effectively in pressure oriented environments to meet scheduled deadlines.

o Capable of interfacing with individuals from diverse cultural backgrounds for enhanced cooperation and rapport.

o Well-developed oral and written communication skills supported by Spanish facility.

o Staff training and development abilities to maximize capital and human resources.

ELECTRONICS
Electronics Specialist

Several years' progressive experience in electronics backed by hands-on technical and quality assurance exposure.

Comprehensive ability to interpret engineering blueprints, shop drawings, schematics, Mil-Spec's and perform associated mathematical calculations.

Extensive troubleshooting and problem solving skills to rapidly identify and resolve component dysfunctions for repair.

Demonstrated orientation to detail is supported by microscopic examination of first articles and use of such specialized equipment as computers, micrometers and optical comparators as well as their calibration.

Sound analytical decision making abilities are backed by scheduling proficiency and overall supervision competence to foster enhanced operational efficiency.

Seasoned ability to use X-ray equipment in addition to strong soldering experience utilizing such materials as gold to repair circuit boards.

Background with lasers, from cadmium to helium including their assembly, alignment, testing and micro-soldering in a clean room environment.

Capable of providing strong leadership to foster enhanced performance, productivity and project commitment.

Interface effectively with all affiliated personnel, from engineering and production, to inspection and quality assurance to further project initiatives.

Well-developed oral and written communication skills are complemented by the ability to provide staff training and development to maximize capital and human resources.

Certified for Optical Systems, NASA-JPL.

Electronics Technician

Over 13 years' experience in electronics backed by extensive training with Control Data Institute.

Comprehensive testing and failure analysis proficiency.

Troubleshooting and problem solving to the component level.

Demonstrated ability to read wiring schematics.

Computer sub-component expertise, involving disc drives, floppys, and a variety of cards.

Familiarity with government specifications and requirements.

Able to efficiently troubleshoot circuit boards.

Capable of utilizing all types of test equipment to test and inspect for circuit board failures.

Familiar with electronic systems for the Navy and Air Force relative to air and ground communications.

Maintenance, repair and replacement of electronic equipment.

Bilingual, fluent in Spanish and English.

Staff training and development of other technicians.

Able to adapt quickly to new organizational settings.

ENGINEER
Automotive Engineer

Over 14 year's responsible experience in automotive service supported by extensive profit and loss experience with positive results.

Senior management experience supported by a significant track record in the international automotive industry.

Extensive hands-on experience in automotive technical service, diagnostics, and repair.

Participative management orientation with particular emphasis on enhanced group dynamics.

Expertise in such areas as order processing, quality control, quality assurance, and customer relations.

Scheduling and master scheduling proficiency for the maximum utilization of human resources.

Comprehensive troubleshooting and problem solving skills with hands-on experience in repair, electrical and electronic diagnosis.

Expertise with latest automotive technology is supported by international application and warranty claims analysis.

Good insights into sales and service operations - can coordinate departments for increased efficiency and profit.

Excellent organizational skills include the ability to handle a variety of challenging assignments simultaneously.

Interface proficiency with upper management, key decision makers as well as Japanese and European representatives.

Interpersonal relations abilities for enhanced rapport and cooperation with technical and service personnel.

Familiar with OSHA safety regulations and hazardous waste

management.

CAD Specialist

Over 18 year's progressive experience in mechanical design supported by a variety of challenging work assignments.

Comprehensive computer and design board skills.

Extensive troubleshooting and problem solving skills.

Demonstrated ability to take products from conceptual stage through final design.

Sound interface skills with research, development, engineering, and sales.

Experience working with close tolerances and government policies and procedures.
Consistently able to meet scheduled deadlines.

Capable of lending insight and making recommendations for equipment fabrication.

Hands-on familiarity with machine shop equipment, including lathes and vertical end mills.

Very good at planning own time and working independently on projects.

Experience includes such diverse assignments as jet engines, diamond lapping machines and plant layouts.

Have designed equipment utilizing exotic metals and plastics, from piping plans to mechanical structures.

Chemical Engineering Candidate

Responsible experience in chemical analysis.

New product formulation proficiency.

Extensive troubleshooting and problem solving skills for production efficiency.

Familiar with chemical and physical testing of polymers. Prepared and documented analysis reports for customers.

Experienced in final inspections and release of compounds.

Demonstrated interpersonal communication skills. Involved in research and development.

Bilingual - fluent in English and Spanish. Staff training and development of two degreed chemists.

Able to adapt quickly to new organizational settings.

Project Engineer

Over 20 years' experience in data communication operations backed by a track record for increasing performance and productivity.

Project scheduling expertise to expedite communication assignments.

Have provided extensive cost estimating recommendations to create a favorable return on investment.

Extensive troubleshooting and problem solving skills for the rapid diagnosis and remedy of system dysfunctions resulting in enhanced system integrity.

Demonstrated ability to perform system analysis from a computer perspective, utilizing such systems as the DEC1170.

Sound supervisory proficiency as demonstrated through staff

scheduling and project management.

Computer competency includes UNIX, DOS, Lotus 123, and Java.

Seasoned personnel skills are indicated through evaluating and promoting activities.

Consistently able to provide technical training and staff development along with recommendations for enhanced system performance.

Capable of meeting scheduled deadlines through time management proficiency as well as production experience.

Familiar with all aspects of hardware and software configurations.

Interface with vendors as well as such internal departments as Production Control, Engineering, Finance, Management and Purchasing to expedite project objectives.

Facilitate staff cooperation and morale through interpersonal skills which emphasize team building.

Dr. Lawrence Peterson

Electrical Engineer

o Hands-on experience in both analog and digital communication systems.

o Knowledge of a variety of computer languages including
Basic, Fortran, Assembly, Intel 8088, and Motorola 6800.

o Design theories include Fourier series for signal analysis - as
well as (FET) Fast Fourier and La Place Transforms for design
and analysis of discreet systems.

o Experience with partial design of transistor tester circuits
in addition to fabrication and subsequent debugging.

o Extensive troubleshooting and circuit diagnosis proficiency
to the component level supported by practical experience
circuit modification for test station applications.

o Competent with all types of electronic test equipment.

o Hands-on experience with new system designs as well as
modifications for enhanced systems performance.

o Expertise with component layout, diagnostic checks, and
system performance evaluations.

o Sound design skills backed by blueprint, wiring schematic,
and technical specifications proficiency to conform to military specifications.

o Scheduling proficiency includes building plans, procurement manifests, in-process analysis, correlation interface,
and Gantt charting for expedient project completions.

o Able to effectively interface with Mechanical Engineers,
Technicians, Contract Administration, Document Control,
Draftsman, Procurement, and Vendors.

o Can assume greater responsibility in a challenging environment through project leadership capability.

Electronics Engineer

Design theories include Fourier series for signal analysis - as well as Fourier, and Fast Fourier Transforms for design and analysis of discrete systems in addition to knowledge of Laplace Transforms for design and analysis of analog systems.

Hands-on experience in digital communication systems, wave shaping circuits, and computer interfacing as well as with the partial design, fabrication and debugging of transistor tester circuits.

Worked with design draftsmen to develop engineering sketches into finished drawings while generating new drawings pertinent to new system designs, changes and modifications for implementation into the production environment.

Developed test procedures for new design modifications to test equipment in addition to developing equipment calibration procedures.

Extensive troubleshooting and circuit diagnosis proficiency to the component level supported by practical experience in circuit modification for test station applications.

Experience with component layout, diagnostic checks, and system performance evaluations.
Sound design skills backed by blueprint, wiring schematic, and technical proficiency to conform to military specifications.

Scheduling proficiency includes procurement manifests, in-process analysis, correlation interface, and Gantt charting for expedient project completions.

Able to effectively interface with Mechanical Engineers, Technicians, Contract Administration, Document Control, Draftsman, Procurement, and Vendors.

Knowledge of a variety of computer languages including Basic, Fortran, Perl, C, and Java.

Staff training abilities include instructing test equipment maintenance.

Electromechanical Engineering

Over 20 year's responsible experience in the diagnosis, test, repair and maintenance of electromechanical systems with a track record for maximizing uptime.

Comprehensive troubleshooting and problem solving expertise to rapidly identify and correct dysfunctions pertinent to motors, controls, safety circuits, automatic start and switching panels as well as gas and diesel engines.

Demonstrated ability to read and interpret electromechanical blueprints and wiring diagrams for AC and DC applications, particularly generator maintenance and repair.

Have fabricated, overhauled, repaired and operationally tested mobile processing center vans associated with power generating systems.

Successfully worked on power generator systems from 60 kilowatt to 600 kilowatt, along with associated equipment and appropriate record keeping.

Sound start-up experience includes research and development as well as sound reporting and documentation proficiency.

Seasoned interface with various computer controlled systems backed by field repairs and custom fabrications for electromechanical modifications.

Consistently able to interface with customers, vendors and contractors to provide technical assistance as well as to expedite project objectives.

Sound supervision proficiency is supported by scheduling and manpower planning experience to meet scheduled deadlines.

Possess the ability to manage large projects as well as multiple projects simultaneously.

Facilities Engineering Director

o Over 10 years varied experience in Facilities Maintenance supported by extensive administrative responsibilities.

o Multi-million dollar budgeting and forecasting proficiency, master planning expertise, and high signature project approval.

o Contract administration expertise includes bid opening, bid approval, capital justifications, cost benefit analysis, and procurement to satisfy project objectives.

o Demonstrated cost reduction proficiency includes inventory control, expense control, staff reorganization and manpower planning for an enhanced return on human resources.

o Large construction and project management experience includes Railroads, Airports, Sewage Plants, Housing, Roads, Bridges and Heating Plants.

o Specific areas of expertise include piping, electrical, cement, fabrication, grading, coordinating utilities, water treatment, as well as releasing permits and documentation.

o Strong maintenance experience with boilers, refrigeration, high voltage, transformers, hazardous materials, and industrial waste.

o Investigated the potential application of co-generation and solar energy to maximize utility objectives.

o Initiated numerous computer programs relative to Maintenance Management, Preventative Maintenance and Quality Assurance, as well as created a film for instructional purposes.

o Comprehensive knowledge of all military specifications regarding construction and facilities maintenance, in addition to general building codes and regulations.

o Facilitate Safety objectives as well as conformance with government specifications through meetings, investigations, and strategic trainings.

o Personnel expertise includes hiring, scheduling, manpower planning, train

Dr. Lawrence Peterson

Fixture Engineer

Over 25 years in jig and fixture building, template and plaster/pattern making, and precision development mechanics.

Demonstrated competency in the use of such precision measuring instruments as height gauges, indicators, transits and levels.

Very competent in use of shop math, as well as proficiency in reading and interpreting blueprints.

Strong layout, fabrication, and optical instrument ability relative to major A.J.'s and sub-assembly fixtures.

Working knowledge and hands-on experience with all types of approved materials: metals, wood, plastic, and composites.

Capable of working from engineering specifications for adherence to close tolerances.

Experience in the modification, overhaul and repair of major aircraft components.

Developed, laid out, and fabricated molded plastic tooling by casting and laminating processes.
Planned, laid out, and fabricated plaster patterns, master molds, and plaster mockups.

Work from M.L.O.'s and engineering data to manufacture various templates and form blocks to engineering drawings.

Produced one-dimensional drawings on decoat and mylar for flat pattern development.

Manufacturing Engineer

o Progressively responsible experience in manufacturing engineering supported by sound supervisory proficiency for improved operational performance.

o Comprehensive technical skills include electronics, from applicable test equipment, lasers and fiber optics, to microwave and digital configurations.

o Extensive troubleshooting and problem solving skills to rapidly identify and correct potential and actual impairments to manufacturing through-put.

o Demonstrated experience with pneumatics, hydraulics, CNC and Programmable Controllers is supported by proficiency with FORTH, PASCAL, Perl, AJAX and FORTRAN.

o Sound accounting competence is bolstered by inventory control, flow charting, routing, Methods Time Measurements, scheduling and productivity audits.

o Seasoned design skills include tooling, machinery and plant layouts for improved product flow, operational efficiency and safety.

o Consistently able to provide workable calculations regarding throughput along with equipment recommendations, methods revisions and personnel training requirements.

o Capable of functioning as a resource person to provide valuable technical assistance to affiliated personnel.

o Familiar with product design feasibility studies as well as new product manufacturing introductions necessitating changes in assembly processes, routing modifications and tooling alterations.

o Interface with a variety of production staff personnel represented by Engineering, Quality Assurance, Manufacturing, Marketing and Accounting.

Manufacturing and Production Engineer

Several years' progressive experience in Manufacturing and Production Engineering with a track record for enhancing operational efficiency.

Comprehensive expertise in machining, plastics, sheet metal, extrusions, die castings and laser optics in addition to knowledge of mechanical, electromechanical and electronics.

Extensive troubleshooting and problem solving skills for the rapid diagnosis and remedy of production and manufacturing dysfunctions.

Demonstrated quality control proficiency includes SQC applications which is further backed by statistical samplings for strict compliance with NASA and Military Specifications.

Sound project scheduling and manpower planning expertise pertinent to new design implementations as well as finished manufactured products to maximize capital and human resources.

Seasoned interface skills with vendors and suppliers pertinent to production, make or buy decisions, design reviews and cost reduction.

Consistently able to function effectively in high production, pressure environments to meet scheduled deadlines.

Capable of initiating effective policies and procedures regarding assembly and various processes related to the manufacture of electromechanical products.

Computer literate with Windows 8, Word, PERFORM and the Cloud.

Professional Engineer

California Registered Professional Electrical Engineer with 19 years responsible experience.

Strong supervisory abilities backed by scheduling and manpower planning expertise for the maximum utilization of human resources.

Large project experience includes interface with contractors, subcontractors.

Administrative skills include writing and evaluating bid proposals as well as precise cost estimating.

Experience in a various settings, from nuclear power plants to steel mills through diverse familiarity with electrical codes and regulations.

Able to interface with Mechanical Engineering, Plant Design, Architects, Civil Engineering, and Production Managers.

Blueprints and wiring schematic and electrical logic diagram proficiency includes system design as well as preparing specifications and calculations for system development.

Proficiency with field installations, maintenance, preventive maintenance, and repair of electrical systems.

Diverse equipment includes motors, transformers, control panels, and instruments with additional skill with high voltage, low voltage, 3 phase, single phase, AC, and DC.

Strong troubleshooting skills for the rapid correction of system dysfunctions as well as reduced operating costs.

Senior Engineer

Over 7 year's responsible experience in Software Engineering supported by Technical Management proficiency.

Comprehensive software research and development skills backed by systems design expertise.
Extensive application analysis sustained by a sound understanding of hardware concepts and operational characteristics.

Strong troubleshooting and problem solving skills to maximize systems performance.
Computer languages include Fortran 77, C, ADA, Pascal, PL/1, JOVIAL, VAX DCL, IBM JCL, IBM Command Language, Basic, COBOL, and software design languages NuMIL and GIST.
Maintain operational systems proficiency relative to VAX VMS, IBM MVS and MVS/XA, UNIX, MS-DOS, and Hewlett-Packard MPE.

Hardware expertise includes VAX 11/785, VAX 8700, IBM 308X, IBM 309X series, Sun workstations, H.P. 3000 Series, and Apollo Workstations, as well as IBM and Macintosh personal computers.

Experience coordinating changes in large software systems to facilitate a smooth transition.

Interface proficiency with management, clients, and all levels of user personnel for enhanced software development and maintenance objectives.

Scheduling competence with PERT and Gantt charts.

Systems Engineer

Over 20 years comprehensive experience in electronics leading to the development of automated system test equipment and system performance analyses.

Extensive troubleshooting and problem solving skills resulting from the review of component, subsystem and system parameters to ensure meeting inherent reliabilities.

Demonstrated master scheduling and manpower planning proficiency in conjunction with project administration skills to maximize capital and human resources.

Sound knowledge of Mil-Specs and applicable standards associated with equipment design, fabrication and testing for enhanced productivity and quality assurance.

Seasoned engineering competence in circuit analysis with emphasis on analog and digital configurations.

Capable of performing effectively in pressure situations to meet program schedules as well as to meet project requirements for development of missile simulation programs.

Strong interface with program office, associate design engineers, manufacturing, and customer personnel to facilitate meeting program and system objectives.

Computer literate with Fortran, Pascal and Basic on DEC VAX and Micro-VAX and PC'S, 1802 Assembly Language, Advanced Continuous Simulation Language, MPS-10 (ADI's AD10 computer language), and EAI's Simstar Translator Computer Language.

Familiar with such analytical tools as SYSL (Dynamic System Analysis & Simulation Software), Program CC (STI's control system software), MatLab, and LOTUS 1-2-3.

Outstanding oral and written communication skills primarily requiring the ability to interpret and explain highly technical operations and procedures.

Department of Defense Security Clearance.

ELECTRICAL
Electrical Specialist

o Hands-on experience with electrical systems encompassing residential, commercial and industrial environments.

o Comprehensive troubleshooting and problem solving skills to rapidly diagnose and remedy system dysfunctions.

o Demonstrated experience with both 120 and 240 VAC single phase wiring is supported by maintenance and preventative maintenance for improved quality assurance.

o Sound installation, modification and repair experience pertinent to power transformers, circuit breakers, switchgear, lights, motors and controls in addition to experience with service disconnects.

o Seasoned rough wiring and finish proficiency on new construction and remodeling's is backed by blueprint and wiring schematic reading proficiency.

o Consistently able to function effectively in pressure situations to meet scheduled deadlines.

General Electrician

Over 7 years of progressive experience in the electrical field supported by strong project proficiency.

Comprehensive bottom line orientation to accomplish assigned tasks within budget requirements.

Extensive troubleshooting and problem solving skills to rapidly diagnose and remedy system dysfunctions.

Reputation for expediently effecting field service and in-house repairs within scheduled parameters.

Demonstrated expertise with AC/DC heavy equipment, programmable controllers, and reliance drive units in addition to instrumentation on recorders and pyrometric equipment.

Sound installation, modification and maintenance experience pertinent to automated equipment in field environments.

Seasoned proficiency in reading blueprints and wiring schematics as well as strong attention to detail for enhanced operational efficiency.

Excellent interpersonal relations abilities for increased rapport and cooperation with customers and co-workers.

Capable of reading blueprints and wiring schematics for prototype development and debugging applications.

Familiar with a wide variety of sensoring devices to facilitate calibration and certification.

Interpersonal skills to facilitate a team atmosphere as well as enhance customer satisfaction.

Staff training and development abilities for the competent repair and maintenance of field equipment.

ESTIMATING
Estimator

Over twenty years' experience in steel supply and fabrication backed by sound estimating and quality control skills.

Comprehensive understanding of machine shop practices, from lathes and end mills to heat treating and laser cutting.

Extensive project management proficiency to minimize bottlenecks and expedite deliveries.

Demonstrated troubleshooting and problem solving skills to enhance the initiation and completion of projects.

Sound inspection and quality assurance abilities, including familiarity with military, AMS, ASTM, and QQ specifications.

Seasoned drafting and blueprint reading proficiency to identify material needs as well as production methods.

Consistently able to develop accurate bid proposals through extensive background and experience in the industry.

Capable of maintaining currency with large and difficult projects through excellent tracking and scheduling skills.

Familiar with virtually all aspects of the materials trade, including mild steels, stainless, aluminum and plastics.

Interface with various organizations to complement existing fabrication operations as well as offer off-site support in such areas as sub-component fabrication.

Facilitate product and project efficiency through currency with the latest fabrication methods as well as materials.

FASHION
Fashion Design Specialist

Over 16 years' experience in design and patternmaking is

backed by extensive troubleshooting and problem solving proficiency relative to art, color, and fabric requirements.

Demonstrated design room competence, to including supervision of artists, patternmakers, cutters, pressers, and sample makers.

Sketch and rendering skills with detailed specifications for patternmaking and sewing.

Seasonal selection and preselecting expertise relative to knit and woven fabrics is supported by experience costing out garments and budgeting prototypes.

Currency with fashion styles and trends for different ages includes maintaining merchandising samples for sales staff.

Strong interface skills with design directors, buyers and sales personnel to promote organizational efficiency.

Facilitated international production assignments, to include detailed specification sheets for manufacturing.

Presentations to corporate merchandising staff relative to design, style, color, and fabric recommendations.

Staff training and development abilities, including strong scheduling skills.

Dr. Lawrence Peterson

FILM
Manager of Film

Several years progressive experience in media promotions backed by advertising, broadcast, and production expertise which can readily be applied to film activities.

Comprehensive management proficiency includes hiring and directing talent as well as project leadership for enhanced efficiency and cost containment.

Extensive troubleshooting and problem solving skills pertinent to writing copy, reviewing storyboards, running proof meetings and monitoring timelines for television and radio.

Demonstrated ability to recommend annual operational and capital budgets, as well as to ensure budget compliance on production operations.

Recommendations to Creative Director with regard to procurement for production services as well as fiscal feasibility.

Seasoned scheduling expertise encompasses personnel, film, radio spots and post production activities.

Routinely obtain permits, certificates of insurance for equipment and locations, and releases from free-lance personnel.

Capable of monitoring complete safety policies and procedures to minimize liability.

Familiar with the various networks in the area with regard to media production, from dubbing to enrichment.

Interface with Directors, Advertising Coordinators, free-lance personnel, municipal representatives and vendors to accomplish production goals.

Facilitate enhanced market penetration through ability to statistically track on-going promotions and advertisements.

Staff training and development abilities include video training presentations.

FINANCE
Financial Specialist

Over 17 years' experience in accounting backed by finance, management, and operational expertise for improved organizational efficiency.

Comprehensive exposure to construction and marketing applicable to a variety of business environments.

Extensive troubleshooting and problem solving skills for the rapid diagnosis and remedy of operational dysfunctions.

Supervision proficiency includes hiring, performance evaluations, scheduling and manpower planning.

Demonstrated expertise in budgeting, forecasting and cash flow management in addition to financial statement development.

Sound accounting proficiency includes computerized payroll, receivables, General Ledger, trust and cost accounting, as well as computerized accounting system initiation.

Solid knowledge of tax and government regulations for enhanced compliance and precision backed by analytical abilities relative to computations and statistics.

Capital justification and acquisition expertise in addition to vendor negotiations and subcontractor coordination.

Capable of functioning effectively in pressure situations to meet scheduled deadlines.

Computer experience with Lotus 1-2-3, Word Perfect, Word, and the IBM 36 operating system.

Well-developed oral and written communication skills with stand-up presentation capability, for enhanced rapport and cooperation with clients and co-workers.

Consistently able to foster enhanced performance, productivity and organizational commitment through staff training and development abilities.

GOLF
Golf Professional

Over 20 years progressive experience in competitive golf with recognition for winning over 70 championship events.

Comprehensive business development proficiency pertinent to Golf Centers, Country Clubs and Convention Centers.

Extensive troubleshooting and problem solving skills relative to such existing and proposed golf facility considerations as leases, land restrictions, environmental studies, water and light studies and size parameters.

Demonstrated public relations abilities pertinent to television commercials, television commentary, and clinics as well as teaching exposure through newspaper and radio.

Sound management proficiency to supervise Pro Shops, golf courses, driving ranges, tournaments and affiliated personnel, including other golf professionals.

Strong organizational skills with regard to grand openings and other promotional events, from staff scheduling to food and beverage coordination.

Consistently able to deal effectively with individuals from diversified cultural backgrounds.

Excellent administrative skills for enhanced profit and los s accountability, particularly in such areas as budgeting, forecasting and projecting.

Well-developed purchasing and merchandising abilities to foster selection, product turnover and profit.

Personnel proficiency in such areas as hiring, scheduling and motivating for enhanced performance, productivity and commitment.

Interface with various men's clubs and civic organizations to augment the visibility of the sport.

GRAPHICS
Graphic Arts

o Over 20 years' experience in graphic art presentations for the entertainment industry with a reputation for successfully meeting creative and challenging media objectives.

o Comprehensive design skills include woodcarvings, silk screening, character aging, character painting, murals, graphics, marble and metal sculpturing.

o Extensive troubleshooting and problem solving skills pertinent to the conceptual development and implementation of multi-media presentations.

o Demonstrated ability to implement creative set environments with minimum information in addition to expertise with color coordination and mix.

o Strong project supervision proficiency in conjunction with manpower planning and scheduling competence to maximize capital and human resources.

o Media settings include television commercials, union and nonunion television and feature presentations, as well as theme park projects for enhanced viewer impact.

o Seasoned interface skills with international production companies represented by such regions as Australia, England, Italy and Canada.

o Consistently recognized for pictorial billboards and unusual, special effects pertinent to scenic presentations.

o Capable of functioning as a contractor and subcontractor to enhance project media initiatives - have worked with numerous commercial production companies.

o Studied under Theodore Lukitz in Los Angeles specializing in multi-media presentations.

Field Coating Inspector

Over 20 years' experience in coating operations.

Comprehensive third party inspection abilities.

Extensive troubleshooting and problem solving skills.

Demonstrated ability to maintain customer specifications.

Sound understanding of a variety of coatings, including baked, polyurethane, epoxy and teflon.

Have performed Spark Tests, and final mil checks to check for pin holes, voids and appropriate coat thickness.

Consistently check equipment and maintain safety data sheets on materials.

Monitor daily activities to determine square footage. Interface skills with customers and contractors.

Outstanding oral and written communication skills. Able to adapt quickly to new organizational settings.

Machine Parts Inspector

Staff training and development experience.

Employee motivation - quality circle competence.

Excellent oral and written communication skills.

Blue print reading proficiency.

Inspection tolerance and equipment familiarity.

Exotic metal (titanium, platinum, waspoloy, aluminum exposure).

Cordax 3 axis measurement, Rockwell - Brinnel hardness testers, veneers, micrometers, height gauges and related equipment.

Supervision experience relative to 10 inspection personnel.

Quality assurance "hot" inspection supervisory experience.

Statistical production control competence.

Strong interface skills with customers relative to proposals.

Analytical troubleshooting and problem solving experience.

Generalist with hands-on experience, from conceptual part stage to final production.

Competent with inspection documentation.

Can operate a variety of material handling equipment.

Am safety conscious and familiar with O.S.H.A. guidelines.

Public Works Inspector

Public Works experience backed by a track record for improving operational efficiency.

Comprehensive inspection skills pertinent to such projects as sewer and storm drains, sidewalks, roads and highways.

Extensive troubleshooting and problem solving skills for the rapid diagnosis and remedy of on-site inspections per specification and standards prior to releasing for delivery.

Demonstrated ability to perform manpower planning and project scheduling for a maximum return on human and fiscal resources.

Pipeline construction experience includes both pressure and gravity configurations.

Soil compaction, asphalt, concrete, and reinforced concrete expertise for application to a variety of project requirements.

Consistently able to supervise General Contractors as well as all work according to prevailing specifications and standards.

Capable of making strategic recommendations to improve operational performance as well as material usage.

In addition to the ability to perform equipment designs, can provide field support for equipment and machinery repairs.

Interface with vendors regarding plant and product inspections.

Strong oral and written communication skills backed by a facility with Spanish.

AUTO
Automobile Insurance Adjuster

Excellent mechanical background lends insight into automobile appraisals, negotiations and facilitates the resolution of liability claims.

Prior automobile adjustment and appraisal experience involving material damage, repair negotiations and subsequent disposition arrangements.

Surveillance expertise to expedite product liability cases.

Background investigating credit card frauds and internal thefts.

Extensive troubleshooting and problem solving abilities.

Seasoned analytical and diagnostic skills for precise case documentation and conclusion.

Well-developed interpersonal abilities to interface effectively with clients, insurance representatives and agencies.

Claims Examiner

Strong analytical decision making proficiency pertinent to the efficient analyses and resolution of Workers' Compensation Claims.

Create Workers' Compensation files, from initial incident through rehabilitation and case resolution.

Extensive troubleshooting and problem solving skills, include auditing for duplicate billings.

Demonstrated ability to assign Investigators to clarify claims, as well as provide recommendations to Attorneys.

Sound interpersonal interface with Physicians, Attorneys, various Vocational Counselors, Insurance professionals and

Claimants.

Seasoned familiarity with Subrogation issues arising from AOE and COE issues.

Consistently able to foster enhanced operational efficiency.

Capable of providing staff training and development.

Training in interpreting medical terminology, as well as permanent disability ratings and vocational rehabilitation.

Outstanding oral and written communication skills backed by proficiency in Russian and German.

Routinely work with individuals from diverse cultural backgrounds.

DESIGN
Interior Design Specialist

Design proficiency includes rendering and 1/8" scale board expertise backed by 3 dimensional modeling.

Insight into restaurant operations which can be leveraged into functional design specifications for enhanced organizational efficiency.

Sales offices and tenant improvements experience.

Experience with electrical plans, reflected ceilings, and display plans.

Expertise with fabrics and color schemes, in addition to space planning proficiency.

Familiar with furniture design particularly current designs and supplier resources.

Interface skills with vendors and sales representatives.

Computer literacy includes spreadsheets and word processing.

Excellent interpersonal skills for enhanced rapport and co-operation with clients and co-workers.

Interior Designer for R.V.'s

o Comprehensive ability to work in residential, commercial, and R. V. settings.

o Extensive space planning abilities supported by well-developed rendering and drafting skills.

o Comprehensive understanding of fabrics, from dying and printing, to floor and window treatments.

o Strong background in tooling relative to cabinet hardware, trimmings, and light accessories.

o Able to take projects from the concept stage to final production to efficiently address client needs.

o Familiar with a variety of different recreational shows for R. V.'s and travel trailers is supported by merchandising proficiency and knowledge of R.V. laws, specifications and 302 codes.

o Interface skills with R.V. dealers as well as ability to perform dealer needs assessments for new product development and customer satisfaction.

o Comprehensive understanding of R.V. price points, available products and potentially new products derived from consumer needs assessments and vendor information.

o Design skills have set industrial trends as well as have impacted on such other industries as furniture design.

o Manufacturing and engineering interface proficiency for enhanced performance, productivity and quality assurance.

o Furniture expertise includes brass accent pieces.

o Interpersonal relations abilities for enhanced rapport and cooperation with clients and staff personnel.

INVENTORY
Inventory Control Specialist

Several years' responsible Management experience to improve performance, productivity and operational efficiency.

Comprehensive understanding of inventory control requirements, including auditing, warehousing, shipping and receiving.

Extensive troubleshooting and problem solving skills pertinent to product distribution and tracings.

Demonstrated ability to initiate policies and procedures for enhanced conformity to company regulations.

Sound computer competence with Ultimate System and Pegasus, in conjunction with inventory control.

Seasoned scheduling and manpower planning abilities to maximize human resources.

Consistently able to handle multiple projects and diverse assignments simultaneously.

Familiar with Military specifications for enhanced conformity and customer satisfaction.

Capable of conducting weekly staff meetings to increase safety and operational integrity.

Analytical decision making abilities applicable to shipping schedules, transportation, and dispatching for on-time deliveries.

Interface with customers, management, trucking personnel, as well as sales and purchasing relative to shipping, receiving and the generation of increased sales opportunities.

Material handling proficiency relative to the systematic

movement and filling of goods.

INVESTIGATION
Personal Injury Investigator

Over 14 years' experience in law enforcement backed by additional experience in accident investigation.

Extensive familiarity with automobile, product liability and personal injury cases.

Thorough understanding of vehicle engineering, crush damage, and the principle direction of force in impacts.

Strong background in math and physics to determine the dynamics of accidents.

State of California Licensed Investigator AQ-11151.

Thorough research skills for precise case documentation and follow-up.

Interface proficiency with attorneys and insurance claim adjusters to establish potential liability.

Video tape abilities for scene analysis to corroborate the physical evidence of accidents.

Seasoned experience researching Federal, State, and local standards as applicable to road hazards and defective highway design.

Capable of interviewing witnesses for establishing credibility for further testimony as well as substantiating case facts.

Computer proficiency - wrote a program to process vehicle scene and deformation data for the verification of impact speeds and automobile behavior.

State of the art 3 dimensional model building expertise to reconstruct accidents and convincingly illustrate true time and motion factors as well as establish liability.

Background investigation to support the key elements of a potential lawsuit in personal injury cases.

LANDSCAPE
Landscape Designer

Several years progressive experience in landscape design and implementation with particular emphasis on drought tolerant, low maintenance, natural landscapes.

Comprehensive landscape exposure includes irrigation, land clearing and plant selection to complement building structures and site configurations.

Extensive project troubleshooting and problem solving skills is supported by scheduling and manpower planning proficiency to maximize capital and human resources.

Demonstrated bidding, contract administration, negotiation, budgeting, forecasting, and projecting expertise in addition to basic accounting, payroll and procurement abilities.

Plant pruning and propagation experience is backed by knowledge of plant pathology, from plant diseases and symptoms to subsequent intervention.

Seasoned experience with climate and functionality assessments for the appropriate utilization of plant materials.

Consistently able to interface with Dealers, Architects, Designers, end users, and Regional Managers to expedite project objectives.

Capable of designing elaborate floral arrangements for special events in addition to experience with waterfalls and specialty planters.

Familiar with all types of garden and landscaping tools, from trenchers and chain saws, to weed eaters and irrigation implements.

Computer literacy is applicable to spread sheets, executive correspondence and design layouts.

Dr. Lawrence Peterson

Landscaping Manager

Over 10 years' experience in ornamental horticulture supported by extensive supervision proficiency.

Landscape development proficiency includes planning, coordinating and implementing major projects.

Budgeting and forecasting abilities encompass profit and loss responsibility, bid proposals, capital justifications.

Extensive troubleshooting and problem solving skills involve managing sub-contractors and landscape personnel.

Sound knowledge of plant pathology, from plant diseases and symptoms to subsequent intervention.

Knowledge of a variety of chemicals including insecticides, fungicides, herbicides and growth regulators.

Interface proficiency with landscape architects for project development.

Expertise with climate and functionality assessments for the appropriate utilization of plant materials.

Interface with vendors and suppliers.

Facilitate presentations to key decision makers relative to landscape renovations, potential projects, and potential problems with ongoing projects.

Ability to utilize landscape to complement building structure features.

Personnel skills include hiring, training, performance appraisals, scheduling, and manpower planning.

Landscape - Irrigation Specialist

Over ten years' experience in landscaping and irrigation.

Demonstrated management supervision abilities.

Commercial and public work projects to $1.8 million.

Rough and finish grading.

Large-scale automatic irrigation systems installation.

Irrigation pumps, mainline and master valve systems.

Familiar with the safe operation and maintenance of a variety of landscaping equipment ranging from backhoes and loaders, to trenchers and augers.

Outstanding oral and written communication skills.

Horticultural expertise, to include specimen trees and hydro seeding.

Outstanding record documentation management.

Sound interface skills with foremen and superintendents.

Purchasing and material delivery coordination.

Staff training and development abilities.

Bilingual - can communicate with Spanish speaking employees.

Extensive troubleshooting and problem-solving skills.

Dr. Lawrence Peterson

LAW
Attorney

Member of the California Bar Association supported by familiarity with legal briefs, memorandum law in motion procedures, estate planning, family law and bankruptcy.

As a Law Clerk, frequently conducted follow-up investigations while researching filed motions, making recommendations with regard to settlement feasibility.

Experience initiating and filing motions for criminal procedure matters as well as drafts for incorporation purposes.

Legal training with an emphasis on Real Estate relative to small builders needs and compliance with applicable regulations.

Management proficiency supported by a strong sales and marketing background as well as seasoned organizational skills.

License in Real Estate is supported by new home sales ranging from condominiums to luxury homes and troubleshooting skills for the quick diagnosis and remedy of legal issues.

Experience in readily determining client needs with an understanding of behavior and motivation patterns is supported by extensive exposure to high dollar projects with its attendant financial impact on client resources.

Extensive analytical research skills that can be applied to the preparation of legal briefs and memoranda.

Capable of conducting investigative follow-up with clients on filed motions and making recommendations for settlement.

Experience delivering weekly meetings to enhance staff commitment and increased productivity.

Private Investigator

Over 13 years in law enforcement backed by several years' experience in insurance investigation.

Comprehensive management and administration skills.

Private Investigators License.

Expertise in claims negotiation.

Extensive troubleshooting and problem solving abilities.

Detail oriented for precise case documentation backed by a clear and precise dictation style.

Demonstrated ability to deal effectively with attorneys, insurance companies, court personnel and adjusters.

Proficient at preparing for and giving court testimony.

Specialized in Workers Compensation cases.

Surveillance experience.

Basic photography and video skills.

Competent in generating monthly reports.

Excellent interpersonal relations abilities able to obtain information from reluctant sources.

Capable of working independently as well as part of a team.

Dr. Lawrence Peterson

Paralegal

Certified Paralegal from an ABA accredited University backed by an extensive academic and business background.

Extensive analytical research skills supported by a sound knowledge of legal procedures, terminology, and an assortment of legal forms.

Familiar with the laws and regulations pertinent to a variety of civil procedures.

Interpersonal relations abilities for enhanced rapport and cooperation with Attorneys, court personnel, clients, witnesses, and coworkers.

Able to function effectively in pressure situations.

Familiar with labor relations, contract disputes, Workers' Compensation, and Risk Management.

Demonstrated management and administration abilities for enhanced troubleshooting and problem solving.

Capable of conducting field investigations including witness and client interviews.

Experience in formal administration hearings includes successful grievance handling.

Strong personnel skills for application to pretrial litigation cases.

Detail oriented, organized, with excellent tracking skills which can be applied to court calendar management.

Strong case management including follow-up accuracy.

Excellent oral and written communication skills - able to deal with people from varied cultural backgrounds.

Principal spokesperson at the annual intra-campus debate

"Moot Court", as well as an active participant in the Paralegal Student's Association.

MACHINING
Machining

Progressive experience in machining supported by the ability to work with a variety of specialized materials, from Kevlar, epoxy, various metals to wood and plaster.

Comprehensive pattern making skills supported by mold making experience applicable to blow molding, rotational molding, vacuum forming and pressure forming.

Have machined composite parts and aluminum molds for aerospace applications.

Experience building prototype parts, forming tools, jigs and fixtures for precise production through such equipment as milling machines, lathes, aluminum and steel TIG and MIG welding.

Extensive troubleshooting and problem solving skills includes making shop sketches for co-workers as well as inspection audits for compliance with strict military specifications.

Demonstrated supervision, scheduling and manpower planning proficiency supported by quality assurance proficiency and shrinkage control.

Sound computer literacy with Fortran and Basic to further machining objectives.

Staff training and development abilities to maximize capital and human resources.

MAINTENANCE
Maintenance and Operations Specialist

Over 20 year's responsible experience in the electrical field backed by sound management proficiency and a license in electrical (general) contracting.

Strong maintenance and preventative maintenance experience includes supervisory proficiency over welders, mechanics, pipe fitters, and electricians to expedite a variety of project concerns.

Large project administrative experience includes budgeting and forecasting abilities supported by purchasing, inventory and cost control, scheduling, and labor relations.

Seasoned troubleshooting and problem solving skills in all areas of electrical repair, including generators, motors, controls, switch gear, AC, DC, high voltage, low voltage, single phase and three phase.

Demonstrated scheduling and manpower planning expertise for the maximum utilization of human resources is backed by strong staff training and development abilities.

Able to read and interpret blueprints, wiring schematics and technical data to perform such project initiatives as the installation of heavy electrical equipment.

Experience installing Environmental Protection Agency related equipment for the Kaiser Steel organization.

Background working with conveyers and such explosive proof equipment as oil submerged breakers.

Experience with electrical support for steam generators, cooling towers, pumps, and battery rooms.

Strong safety orientation for CAL-OSHA compliance - have given numerous presentations on specialized topics.

Able to rebuild and repair large generators, motors, and cranes, as well as related instruments.

Superintendent of Maintenance

Several years' progressive experience providing responsible building-related services to County departments with emphasis on sound management and administration.

Comprehensive operating proficiency includes profit and loss account ability, budgeting, forecasting, and projecting in addition to performance analysis on existing projects.

Proven management competence includes scheduling, manpower planning and manpower utilization to maximize capital and human resources.

Extensive troubleshooting and problem solving skills to rapidly diagnose and remedy project dysfunctions.

Demonstrated ability to inspect buildings and grounds in conjunction with maintenance and preventative maintenance parameters while determining needs for alterations and improvements.

Supervisory proficiency regarding large and unique projects with additional expertise in interfacing with affiliated department personnel to ensure quality and schedule integrity.

Seasoned ability to prepare budgets and initiate material and labor estimates while interpreting building plans with regard to feasibility and complexity.

Consistently able to prepare and present project findings and required alterations regarding capital improvement programs and facility reconstruction initiatives.

Extensive knowledge of building trades, from carpentry and plumbing to air conditioning and electrical systems, with particular attention given to system integration.

Interface with OSHA, Architects, California South Coast Air Quality Management District, State Department of Water Resources and labor representatives to audit existing and proposed regulatory initiatives.

Maintenance Engineering

Over 17 year's responsible experience in production backed by strong supervisory abilities.

Extensive maintenance and preventative maintenance experience for enhanced up-time, particularly with boiler and refrigeration units.

Able to read and interpret blueprints, wiring schematics and technical data to achieve project objectives.

Seasoned electrical troubleshooting and problem solving, including controls and motors.

Demonstrated scheduling and manpower planning expertise is backed by strong staff training and development abilities for the maximum utilization of human resources.

Capital justification experience for large purchases.

Extensive food processing and conveying equipment experience includes fabrication, installation and maintenance.

Work well under the pressures associated with fast paced environments.

Familiar with sanitary welding, fabrication, as well as hydraulics.

Strong safety orientation in following OSHA guidelines.

Programming experience with T.I. Controllers.

Interface with production, packaging, processing, and parts personnel for enhanced performance.

Production Maintenance

Experienced in general machine production maintenance.

Repair welding - arc and gas.

Automotive repairs - trucks, fork-lifts, hydraulics.

Compressors, large process vacuum equipment.

Boilers (steam, water) up through medium pressure.

Repair and maintenance of boiler controls.

Electronics - clean room operations.

Maintenance and repair of high micron filter systems.

Exotic gas plumbing - installation of ventilation systems including alarm systems.

Installation, maintenance and repair of HVAC systems. Safety and fire protection systems.

Facility engineering and plant layout. Familiar with O.S.H.A. regulations.

Experienced in staff training and development.

Computerized maintenance record keeping.

Knowledge of inventory control systems.

Understanding of electrical and electronic systems. Blue print reading - schematic reading.

MARKETING
Marketing Analyst

Facilitate extensive marketing activities to expedite the sale of computer data to outside firms for demographic exploitation.

Computer proficiency includes computerized planogram s, competitive price and product analysis, and merchandise tracking for both seasonal and special promotion applications.

In addition to senior management, interface activities include merchandising, sales representatives, MIS department, as well as food brokers and food manufacturers.

Work closely with information companies such as A.C. Nielsen, research companies, and marketing firms in generating critical data for future product impact.

Possess basic C programming proficiency with personal and mainframe systems as well as Word, SAS, and Lotus 1-2-3 expertise.

Perform service estimates and proposals as well as create specific programs for marketing information companies to generate custom surveys and print outs from on-going facility purchasing histories.

Provide input regarding future product selections which potentially will increase profit and volume yields.

Possess strong demographic skills for increased market penetration.

Several years' responsible experience in management supported by such administrative abilities as budgeting, forecasting, and projections.

Extensive troubleshooting and problem solving skills for enhanced organizational efficiency.

Procurement and inventory control expertise is supported by grand opening and remodeling expertise-Personnel skills include hiring, training, and development.

MEDICAL
Assistant Head Nurse

Over 8 years' providing quality healthcare to Labor, Delivery, Medical and Surgical Units.

Working towards MSN in Administration at Dominguez Hills.

Supervisory proficiency as a Charge Nurse, Head Nurse and Shift Coordinator.

Demonstrated knowledge of the principles and practices related to team nursing and primary care nursing.

Ability to coordinate and motivate an effective healthcare staff, as well as serve as resource person.

Prepared studies and implemented changes in Labor and Delivery, to include an Orientation Program and Perinatal Nurse Program.

Familiar with birthing procedures to include caesarean, bilateral tubal ligations as well as labor and delivery.

Interface with physicians and other of medical staff for enhanced organizational efficiency.
Extensive troubleshooting and problem solving skills.

Competent at evaluating symptoms, reactions and intervention steps to provide effective patient care.

Experience Categorizing patients based on acuity for staffing purposes.

Experience attending to physiological, psychological and

environmental factors affecting the patient.

Dr. Lawrence Peterson

Manager of Medical Billing

Several years' responsible supervisory experience in medical billing supported by expertise with electronic billing systems.

Strong troubleshooting and problem solving skills to resolve account issues and personnel dysfunctions.

Analytical decision making abilities for workable solutions for operational and administrative dysfunctions.

Personnel abilities include hiring, training, and staff development as well as management meetings for increased productivity and commitment.

Computer proficiency includes DOMS 2 utilizing SAFTER software, Texas Instruments Business System 300A using Poorman Douglas Corporations Medical Computer Solutions Software, and related peripheral equipment.

Data processing abilities relative to generating reports, billing insurance and statement forms, posting payments, and sending Medicare claims electronically.

Accounting abilities include Receivables, Payables, Payroll, Cash Receipts, Collections, and all banking duties, including posting and deposits.

Proficiency with diagnosis and ICD coding.

Familiar with such insurance companies as Blue Shield, Medicare, Medi-Cal, and HMO/PPOs - implemented Magnetic Tape billing for Medicare and Medi-Cal patients.

Interface expertise with all levels of management, staff, and clients for enhanced rapport and cooperation.

Demonstrated ability to interface with individuals from various cultures and backgrounds through French, German, and Spanish language proficiency.

Routinely initiate policies and procedures for enhanced organizational efficiency.

Manager of Respiratory Therapy

Several years' progressive experience in Respiratory Therapy backed by strong supervision proficiency for adult and neonatal applications.

Comprehensive technical expertise in such areas as pulmonary rehabilitation, blood gas analysis, trauma and intensive care, arterial puncture, home care and physical assessments.

Extensive equipment troubleshooting and problem solving skills supported equipment recommendations as well as staff and patient training.

Demonstrated ability to function effectively in pressure environments pertinent to such applications as Emergency Room operations, Code Blue conditions and floor operations.

Sound business competence is reflected by budgeting, forecasting and projecting experience for improved operational control and effectiveness.

Seasoned supervision proficiency in addition to strategic recommendations for improved performance, productivity and client care.

Consistently able to interface with patients, patients' families, Nurses, Doctors, Paramedics and affiliated medical personnel.

Capable of assuming positions of increased responsibility as well as providing on-going training for purposes of staff development.

Management Service Coordinator

Over nine year's progressive experience in the medical field supported by management proficiency and a track record for improving operational control.

Comprehensive supervision skills include scheduling, manpower planning, payroll verification, and instructional presentations to foster enhanced compliance with stated objectives.

Extensive troubleshooting and problem solving skills pertinent to such accounting functions as billing, collections, account follow-ups, insurance eligibility, posting and deposits.

Demonstrated competence with CPT-4 and ICD-9 coding, as well as with computer and manual insurance billing systems, in addition to expertise with Medicare, Medi-Cal, Workman's Compensation and private insurance.

Experience with receivables in excess of $1.6 million per month in conjunction with an average collection rate of 80 to 90% in as little as 75 days.

Seasoned data processing abilities relative to report generation, billing insurance and statement forms, posting payments, and sending Medicare claims electronically.

Consistently able to foster enhanced performance, productivity and staff commitment through strategic interpersonal leadership skills.

Fast learner capable of assuming positions of greater responsibility requiring the coordination of diverse tasks and assignments with tight deadlines.

Interface effectively with patients, doctors, insurance providers and affiliated personnel to increase rapport and co-operation.

Facilitate improved operational efficiency through on-going recommendations and policy initiation.

Nurse

Several years responsible experience in nursing with an extensive background in Neonatal Intensive Care supported by supervisory proficiency as a Charge Nurse and Shift Coordinator.

Extensive knowledge of nursing principles and practices related to team nursing and primary care nursing.

Administrative expertise includes budgeting, inventory control, and cost control proficiency.

Purchasing experience includes interfacing with vendors to secure bids and proposals on necessary equipment and supplies.

Strong organizational skills with the ability to effectively coordinate daily hospital operations.

Able to interface with Doctors, hospital personnel, and other Nurses to enhance rapport and team work.

Extensive healthcare troubleshooting and problem solving skills for enhanced organizational efficiency.

Interpersonal relations abilities for increased cooperation with patients and distressed relatives.

Scheduling proficiency for the maximum utilization of human resources.

Personnel skills include hiring, training, development, performance appraisals, disciplinary actions, as well as authoring policies and procedures.

Dr. Lawrence Peterson

Public Health Specialist

Over 12 years in educational activities, backed by academic training and practical experience in public health.

Sound analytical decision making abilities and organizational proficiency for enhanced program development.

Familiar with leading practices, philosophies, and strategies for the successful implementation of progressive health education policies and procedures.

Successfully developed a Pacific-oriented health education program while at Papua New Guinea.

Facilitated health education programs at the Palama low-income settlement involving summer school and community programs.

Extensive lecture presentations relative to staff training and curriculum development, including lectures to Nursing students.

Versatile teaching methods - able to present the fundamentals of health education from a variety of academic perspectives.

Demonstrated interpersonal relations skills, including well-developed oral and written communication proficiency.

Radiologist Technologist

Over 20 years' experience in radiologic services including hospital radiology department management and technical support.

Comprehensive background in diagnostic radiology services to ensure quality support of patients while maintaining conformance to government and health guidelines.

Extensive troubleshooting and problem solving skills to discharge the necessary maintenance of radiology standards in compliance with Joint Commission on Accreditation of Hospital requirements.

Demonstrated proficiency in planning, directing, and coordinating radiologic services within established budgets to maximize capital and human resources.

Sound knowledge of the technical aspects of radiation safety in a hospital environment to enforce policies and procedures adopted regarding radiation hazards and control.

Seasoned advisor to academia for radiology technology programs is supported by stand-up presentations to investigate and further health and operational initiatives.

Consistently foster team cooperation and leadership to promote additional performance, productivity and commitment to established quality standards.

Capable of participating in long range planning for new facilities, including capital justifications, equipment procurement, manpower planning and scheduling requirements.

Equipment maintenance and preventative maintenance is supported by proficiency for implementing immediate repairs and an effective inventory.

Interface proficiency with hospital administrators, medical staff, and patients for enhanced radiologic service performance, cooperation and rapport.

Well-developed oral and written communication skills are supported by Spanish fluency as well as staff training competence to further functional goals.

Dr. Lawrence Peterson

Radiation Therapist

15 years' experience in Radiation Therapy Technology.

Comprehensive grasp of medical terminology.

Equipment familiarity includes Varian Clinac 4,6-100,18, Seimans 6, EMI Rotational 4, and ortho-voltage units.

Extensive troubleshooting and problem solving skills.

Supervision skills for enhanced staff motivation.

Ability to get complicated concepts across to students.

Sound spatial skills for therapeutic treatment planning.

Equipment maintenance, troubleshooting and simple repairs.

Capable of identifying training needs and heading meetings.

Facilitate "high tech" and "high touch" integration.

Outstanding oral and written communication skills.

Registered Nurse

Over 20 years' experience in Nursing supported by expertise in Mental Health and Chemical Dependency.

Nursing background includes Medical, Surgical, Oncology, Pediatrics Recovery, and Orthopedics.

Extensive knowledge of nursing principles and practices.

Supervisory experience includes Charge Nurse proficiency.

Extensive problem solving skills for emergency care.

Demonstrated ability to maintain patient confidentiality.

Facilitates on-going Alcoholic and Narcotics Anonymous treatment principles, and other 12 step programs.

Provide emotional support for patients diagnosed with catastrophic illnesses and cancer disfiguring surgeries.

Can provide group counseling on the medical aspects of chemical dependency with patients as well as their families.

Seasoned interpersonal relations abilities to enhance rapport with patients and co-workers.

Interface skills with physicians, psychiatrists, counselors, and other mental health personnel for improved healthcare.

Able to manage assaultive patient behavior.

Staff training and development abilities.

Respiratory Therapist

Six years' experience in Respiratory Therapy Care with experience and qualifications in the following areas:

Set-up of durable medical equipment in conjunction with CPR training for neonatal and pediatric monitoring with actual patient contact for on-going patient monitoring and clinical updates.

Record and transmit pertinent data for transcription of two-channel pneumograms to determine subsequent monitor dependence.

Provide in-service instruction to nurses and physicians regarding such new equipment applications as home ventilators, oxygen saturation monitors, apnea - bradycardia monitors, and feeding pumps.

Possess specialized knowledge in the various adult, pediatric and neonatal modalities of respiratory care.

Routinely provide strategic recommendations for equipment and therapeutic applications resulting in improved cardio-pulmonary health.

Participate in an on-going research project pertinent to billing and physiological data recording as well as subsequent analyses for enhanced compliance with insurance requirements.

Interface with vendors for supplies, capital equipment negotiations and custom equipment applications.

Marketing experience includes the ability to open new accounts as well as service existing accounts.

Can identify potential equipment applications for enhanced account development.

Outstanding oral and written communication skills for enhanced rapport and cooperation with clients and medical personnel.

Staff training and development abilities for improved performance, productivity and commitment.

Staff Nurse

Over 20 years responsible experience in nursing backed by experience in intensive care, neurology, trauma, and open heart surgery.

Extensive charge nurse experience in critical care delivery supported by nurse training and development.

ACLS Certified, Registered Nurse II - License No. J313333, NY 306634, currently preparing for CCRN exam.

Pre and post-operative open heart experience was part of an original open heart surgery team.

Extensive healthcare troubleshooting and problem solving skills, including providing emotional and psychological support to patients and families.

Demonstrated ability to conduct physical assessments and make recommendations for follow up monitoring.

Provide in-patient education regarding a variety of treatment modalities, including preceptoring of graduate and student nurses.

Monitor laboratory values as well as provide monitoring and troubleshooting of such invasive equipment as pulmonary artery catheters.

Serve on committees to provide recommendations and strategies for improving the quality of healthcare.

Interface proficiency with Doctors, hospital personnel and other Nurses to enhance rapport and team work.

Dr. Lawrence Peterson

X-Ray Technician

o Comprehensive knowledge of x-ray equipment and procedures.

o Communicate effectively with patients to insure a full understanding of exam procedures.

o Demonstrated ability to maintain patient confidentiality.

o Interpersonal skills to enhance patient relaxation.

o Understanding of X-Ray department from front office to back.

o Interface proficiency with Doctors, Nurses, Technicians, and other hospital personnel.

o Licensed in CRT, ARRT and Fluoroscopy.

o Placed 2nd for exhibit at 1989 CSRT.

o Member of ARRT, CSRT, and Inland Valley District.

MANUFACTURING
Manufacturing Design Specialist

Over 20 years' experience in the design and production of composite assemblies for advanced aeronautical systems.

Comprehensive background developing of manufacturing tooling and processes for assurance of design production.

Extensive troubleshooting and problem solving skills to correct identified defects during manufacturing to optimize production efficiency.

Demonstrated master scheduling and manpower planning proficiency to maximize capital and human resources.

Consultant to Design Engineering on composite structural members and bonded components to facilitate the manufacture of unique designs.

Sound knowledge of Mil-Specs and applicable standards associated with composite materials and production processes for enhanced productivity and quality assurance.

Capable of performing manufacturing capability, engineering production and trade-off studies in support of design for cost minimization.

Familiar with DoD aeronautical system general proposal requirements to provide extensive inputs for major system procurement.

Interface proficiency with management, subcontractor, and customer personnel to facilitate program performance.

Well-developed oral and written communication skills in conjunction with stand-up presentations expertise.

Staff training and development of manufacturing engineers for enhanced utilization of human resources.

Department of Defense Security Clearance with EBI.

Manufacturing Engineering

o Over 19 years responsible experience in Engineering supported by comprehensive management proficiency.

o Administrative abilities include budgeting, forecasting, and projections.

o Capital justifications as well as such other Industrial Engineering functions as MTM, cost reduction, staging, routing and flow charting.

o Scheduling and manpower planning expertise for the maximum utilization of human resources.

o Troubleshooting and problem solving skills to eliminate project dysfunctions as well as adhere to critical military specifications.

o Diversified machine shop expertise in addition to extensive exposure to aircraft structures, communications satellites, reciprocating and centrifugal pumps, valves, and machine tools.

o In addition to proficiency with blueprints and wiring schematics, possess a background in design, manufacturing processes and such production support functions as tooling.

o Have initiated and written detailed planning instructions for machine parts, sheetmetal parts, composites, and assemblies.

o Material knowledge encompasses steel, aluminum, plastics, composites, and a variety of exotic metals.

o Research and Development experience, from the conceptual stage to full scale mock-ups.

o Interface with Design Engineering, Industrial Engineering, Machine Shop, Procurement, and Contract Administration to expedite project initiatives.

o Material Review Board experience as well as Quality Assurance for enhanced product performance and integrity.

o Computer proficiency includes 2D & 3D graphic systems.

Production Manager

Strong supervision skills backed by seasoned administrative abilities.

Comprehensive production management skills relative to budgeting, forecasting, production analysis, and scheduling.

Extensive troubleshooting and problem solving skills.

Demonstrated purchasing and inventory control abilities, including proficiency with MRP systems.

Sound computer skills relative to management information systems and other proprietary programs.

Interface proficiency with production control, vendors, engineering, finance, management and purchasing.

Consistently able to meet scheduled deadlines through effective management and diagnostics.

Capable of assuming greater responsibility for profit and loss activities.

Working catalyst coordinating defense contract audit agencies with General Dynamics relative to material acquisition, production control, and weapons specifications.

Facilitate procurement for such products as electro-mechanicals, sealants, major electrical, castings and raw material.

Outstanding oral and written communication skills.

Production and Shipping Supervisor

Several years' responsible experience in supervision backed by both production and shipping proficiency.

Comprehensive understanding of inventory control requirements, including auditing, warehousing, shipping and receiving.

Extensive troubleshooting and problem solving skills to initiate practical, cost-effective solutions to organizational dysfunctions.

Demonstrated competence for handling diverse assignments as well as multiple projects simultaneously.

Sound analytical decision making abilities relative to shipping schedules, transportation and dispatching for on-time deliveries.

Start-up expertise includes site location, capital justifications and facilities layout.

Capable of working effectively in pressure environments to meet scheduled deadlines.

Familiar with all warehouse equipment, from forklifts and reach trucks, to order pickers and power jacks.

Material handling proficiency for the efficient movement and filling of goods.

On-going staff meetings to promote policy and safety awareness in addition to improved compliance with operational initiatives.

Staff training and development abilities include scheduling and manpower planning expertise for the maximum utilization of human resources.

Can make recommendations for material substitutions and

manpower capabilities relative to manufacturing feasibility.

MANAGEMENT
Boat Manager

Over 16 year's progressive experience in marine service backed by management proficiency for enhanced organizational efficiency.

Capable of performing budgeting, forecasting, projecting, estimating and contract negotiations, as well as capital justifications.

Comprehensive supervision skills include hiring, training and scheduling technical personnel to meet challenging service requirements.

Extensive diagnostic troubleshooting and problem solving skills applicable to inboard, outboard, I/O, and jet boat configurations.

Service, repair and maintenance experience on customer units ranges from small pleasure boats to sport yachts.

Analytical decision making abilities include sound warranty claim handling and interface with satellite stores to resolve manufacturer and customer service problems.

Seasoned maintenance and preventative maintenance abilities are backed by extensive knowledge of Parts Department requirements.

Consistently encourage safety and quality assurance to enhance employee morale as well as customer satisfaction.

Capable of facilitating manufacturing objectives, from setting the back-log to scheduling fabrication and assembly.

Wrote Flat Rate Manual for technician commission schedules as well as numerous policies and procedures for enhanced operational efficiency.

Staff training and development abilities include in-house seminars for such applications as warranty problems.

Able to adapt quickly to new organizational settings and work effectively in fast-paced, pressure oriented environments.

Concrete Manager

Over 12 years combined experience in Management, Operations and Quality Assurance is effectively supported by a track record for significantly improving operational efficiency.

Comprehensive operational expertise includes profit and loss accountability, budgeting, forecasting, projecting and expense control to maximize profitability.

Extensive troubleshooting and problem solving skills to rapidly diagnose and remedy operational and organizational dysfunctions.

Demonstrated interface proficiency with management, key decision makers and affiliated personnel to further organizational policies and objectives as well as to augment account revenue.

Sound analytical decision making abilities supported by scheduling, master scheduling, manpower planning and manpower utilization to maximize capital and human resources.

Seasoned interpersonal communication skills supported by stand-up presentation proficiency for enhanced cooperation and rapport in meeting forecasted goals.

Consistently able to function effectively in pressure situations to meet scheduled deadlines as well as to expediently handle crisis situations.

Capable of hiring, evaluating, training and motivating staff personnel for enhanced performance, productivity and organizational commitment.

Experience successfully managing large projects as well as presiding over Quality Control to emphasize quality, safety and customer satisfaction.

Seasoned collective bargaining skills include interface with management and union personnel for enhanced cooperation and rapport.

Well-developed oral and written communication skills are supported by computer experience to optimize data processing objectives.

Hotel Manager

Twenty years generalist experience in the hotel industry backed by expertise in Hotel Management and Administration.

Certified Hotel Administrator (C.H.A.) backed by additional training in hotel management and practices.

Extensive troubleshooting and problem solving skills for enhanced operational control and return on investment.

Expertise in hotel renovation, planning and construction, including public area improvements and hotel openings, as well as possess significant International exposure.

Demonstrated sales and marketing abilities result in a substantial increase in room occupancy, average rate, and guest satisfaction.

Skilled communicator and administrator for enhanced team relations and task fulfillment.

Staff training and development, including the revision of operation manuals and the development of training programs.

Operational and administrative control of Food and Beverage, Housekeeping, Front Office, Bell Service, Security, and Reservations departments.

Proficient in budgeting, forecasting and a maximum return on manpower resources.

Multilingual, fluent in English, French, and Arabic for improved communication and client rapport.

Strong academic background in marketing and hotel management for increased market penetration.

Sound analytical decision making skills for business development and organizational efficiency.

Capable of assuming greater responsibility in a high volume hotel environment.

Manager of Bus Lines

Over 20 year's responsible experience in management supervision backed by MBO and administrative proficiency.

Profit and loss responsibility includes budgeting and forecasting competence.

Sound analytical abilities for strategic decision making and workable solutions to organizational dysfunctions.

Working knowledge and experience with Toyota Production System TQA, Kaizen and Hejunka principles.

Adept in all areas of distribution and warehouse operations for maximum efficiency and profitability.

Managed material and production control activities in 3 different manufacturing environments, from healthcare products to printed circuit boards in high volume settings.

MRP inventory control expertise in addition to master scheduling, capacity planning, and shop floor control.

Shipping and Receiving background including customized shipping schedules and knowledge of modes of transportation.

In addition to staff training and development, possess scheduling and manpower planning competence.

Capital justification, purchasing, and cost benefit analysis experience for a high return on investment.

Comprehensive marketing abilities include bid proposals, market data analysis and demographics.

Extensive troubleshooting and problem solving skills for improved organizational efficiency.

Interface with Quality Control, Accounting, Engineering, and Service Maintenance.

Interpersonal relations abilities for enhanced rapport and cooperation with customers and personnel.

Property Manager

Over 10 year's responsible experience in supervision and administration backed by strong operations expertise.

Comprehensive marketing abilities for enhanced sales and product - service development.

Extensive troubleshooting and problem solving skills for improved organizational efficiency.

Real estate expertise relative to new site selections, developments, refurbishings and lease agreements.

P & L responsibility supported by enhanced sales, new contracts and the successful expansion of a new territory.

Supplied input recommendations for run profitability between terminal facilities.

Experienced in developing cost control programs for an enhanced return on equity.

Sound analytical abilities for strategic decision making and workable solutions to organizational dysfunctions.

Scheduling and manpower planning competence for the efficient utilization of human resources, including staff training and development abilities.

Union interface skills including agreements, grievances and arbitration.

Set pay incentives to enhance staff motivation as well as establish regional personnel policies and procedures.

Outstanding oral and written communication skills, including fluency in both English and Spanish.

Overall public contract responsibility relative to OCTD and DASH transit systems.

Nursing Home Manager

Over 20 years progressive experience in the health care industry backed by a significant track record for facilitating strategic business turnarounds.

Administrative expertise includes profit and loss accountability, budgeting, cash flow management, projections, forecasting, and cost reduction experience.

Operational skills are pertinent to such business dynamics as scheduling, purchasing and cash control.

Extensive troubleshooting and problem solving skills for the expedient resolution of organizational dysfunctions resulting in enhanced performance and productivity.

Personnel proficiency encompasses hiring, training, staff evaluations, policy and procedure initiation, and staff development for greater operational commitment.

Strong master scheduling and manpower planning skills for expedient task accomplishment as well as to maximize capital and human resources.

Business development expertise includes capital justifications, competitive bids, estimating, quotes, accounts receivables and payables.

Sound analytical abilities for strategic decision making as well as to maintain quality assurance objectives through strategic policy initiation.

Grant and proposal administration proficiency is supported by interpersonal negotiations with banks and financial institutions to gain organizational funding.

Interpersonal relations abilities for enhanced rapport and cooperation with specialized populations as well as physicians, nurses and affiliated medical personnel.

Legislative interaction with the Department of Health to initiate critical programs relative to developmentally disabled populations residing in nursing home facilities.

Property Manager

Responsible experience in property management is backed by multiple unit operations, rentals, collections, evictions, and auditing client accounts.

Comprehensive analytical decision making abilities in conjunction with extensive troubleshooting and problem solving skills for increased organizational efficiency.

Operational proficiency includes Profit and Loss accountability, budgeting, forecasting, and bid proposal negotiations.

Familiar with the current laws and regulations regarding rent control and leasing transactions as well as eviction requirements.

Demonstrated accounting skills include payables, receivables, General Ledger, payroll, inventory control, and collections.

Sound scheduling, manpower planning and coordinating expertise relative to maintenance, repair services, and inspections to maximize human and capital resources.

Seasoned interpersonal relations abilities for enhanced rapport and cooperation with clients and co-workers.

Capable of interfacing with city, county, state and federal representatives as well as with individuals from diverse cultural backgrounds.

Property management skills are applicable to commercial and industrial settings.

Computer literate with Windows 8, Cloud, Lotus 1 -2-3, Word

and QuickBooks.

Dr. Lawrence Peterson

MODELING
Performing Artist

Currently working as an understudy in the play "Beauty Shop" as a major character.

Was featured in "E.O.B. Nixon" and "Committed" through the Bill Dance Casting Agency.
Experience co-reading for Hollywood Theatrical Studios.

Have experience applying my theatrical skills to such settings as photography sessions, modeling, commercials and the theatre.

Am very fashion conscious and can adapt to a variety of fashion roles - was hostess for an Ebony Fashion Fair and won a trophy for modeling in Chicago.

Traveled extensively on singing engagements and was featured at the Playboy Club and at the Pacifica Hotel.

Am 5' 10" tall, a size 10, and am very photogenic.

Very athletic, enjoy horseback riding, roller skating, tennis, aerobics, jogging, and bicycling to maintain fitness.

Can play roles ranging from age 25 on up and enjoy challenging character parts.

Model

Experience with photo sessions for enhanced media impact.

Have performed improvisations in a variety of roles.

Excellent cold and cue card reading proficiency.

Make-up skills for dramatic appearance.

Can adapt to varied wardrobe requirements.

Outstanding auditioning techniques.

Training in camera dynamics and posing.

Acting proficiency for effective role presentation.

Can perform a variety of roles and characters.

Am very photogenic and quickly adapt to new settings.

Physical features: 5' 7", 115 pounds, brown eyes and hair.

Experience performing for doubles and singles commercials.

Volunteer acting work with Universal Studios.

Outstanding oral and written communication skills.

Excellent physical fitness and recreational aptitude.

OFFICE
Office Manager

Over 6 years responsible experience with payables, receivables is supported by extensive office management.

Comprehensive analytical skills include project tracking and prioritization abilities to coordinate a variety of on-going assignments simultaneously.

Strong attention to detail is effectively supported by extensive troubleshooting and problem solving skills to rapidly diagnose and remedy organizational dysfunctions.

Able to audit accounts and funds, prepare monthly budgets, reconcile accounts, and prepare payroll records, invoices, time records, requisitions and purchase orders.

Sound personnel proficiency encompasses hiring, training, staff evaluations, policy initiation and staff development for greater organizational commitment.

Capable of working independently or as a team player in high pressure environments to expedite project initiatives.

Proficient with Word, Insight, QuickBooks, LOTUS 1-2-3, Works and QUEST Inventory System.

Experience with a complete computerized accounting system, including General Ledger, Accounts Receivable and Accounts Payable.

Interpersonal skills include interface with individuals from diverse cultural backgrounds for improved team dynamics and customer satisfaction.

Office Support Specialist

Comprehensive analytical decision making abilities are supported by extensive troubleshooting and problem solving skills to rapidly diagnose and remedy customer service dysfunctions.

Demonstrated ability to function effectively in pressure situations to expedite assignments and scheduled deadlines.

Seasoned organizational competence in addition to a strong attention to detail for precise record keeping.

Knowledge of Data Base, Word, LOTUS 1 -2-3,, Windows 8 and Cloud technology.

Capable of applying leadership and interpersonal communication proficiency for increased rapport and cooperation with customers and co-workers.

Interface competency with management, key decision makers, coworkers and individuals from diverse cultural backgrounds.

Facilitate a variety of challenging projects simultaneously through strong prioritization and coordination skills.

Have successfully assumed positions of increased responsibility.

OPERATIONS
Operations Specialist

Over 9 year's responsible experience in building a business.

Comprehensive sales and marketing proficiency for enhanced volume and repeat accounts.

Extensive troubleshooting and problem solving skills.

Demonstrated management and administration skills, from supervision to billing and insurance.

Business start-up skills; built a firm from the ground up through the opening of a new territory.

Seasoned budgeting, forecasting & cost reduction expertise.

Consistently able to establish excellent rapport with customers for numerous referrals.

Capable of opening new territories and launching new products.

Numerous letters of recommendation from satisfied customers.

Possess initiative, high energy, and am willing to go the extra mile to secure new business.

Interface with a variety of personnel to satisfy customer needs and requirements.

Have made numerous presentations and demonstrations, from leading automobile dealerships to the Department of Navy.

Display the ability to make sound decisions for enhanced business development.

Outstanding oral and written communication skills.

Staff training and development abilities.

Willing to relocate to secure new business.

OPTICS
Optics Specialist

Over 16 years' experience in laser optics.

Comprehensive metal mirror fabrication expertise.

Extensive troubleshooting and problem solving skills.

Demonstrated ability to adhere to close tolerances.

Sound optical testing and alignment proficiency.

Certified Welder experienced with laser welding, cutting and heat-treating.

Consistently able to meet scheduled deadlines.

Capable of performing rigorous quality control.

Experience with copper, molybdenum, stainless steel, chrome, and nickel, as well as ULE, BK7 and Quartz glass.

Interface with engineering to insure specifications.

Facilitate production and machine shop operations.

Gold electroplate experience on mirror surfaces, as well as ran vapor deposit coating machines.

Focus modules and beam delivery fabrication, including laser scanning systems and power meters.

PAINTING
Auto Painter

Complete knowledge of preparation of damaged auto's - trucks.

Ability to apply a variety of special paint mediums.

Competence with micro fische formula specifications.

Color matching, blending and touch-up.

Wood grain applications and pin stripe detailing.

Minor body and mechanical repair.

Adept at lacquer application and finishing.

Training and staff development skills.

Experience with all types of spray equipment.

Volume oriented - high production for high turnover.

Quality control and assurance oriented.

Competent in expense control resulting in greater profits.

Perform routine maintenance on equipment which reduces replacement costs.

PERSONNEL
Human Resources Manager

Several years responsible experience in human relations backed by a track record for initiating major policies and procedures to accomplish short and long-range operating objectives.

Senior division management proficiency with a major corporation to promote the manpower efficiency of up to 1700 personnel in domestic and non-domestic locations.

Multi-million dollar budget expertise includes fixed and controllable expenses, as well as forecasting and projecting experience to meet stated objectives.

Extensive troubleshooting and problem solving skills regarding strategic planning, operational performance review, and legal issues for such case considerations as EEO and ERISA.

Demonstrated ability to recruit and train effective staff personnel to complement future divisional requirements as well as overall company objectives.

Innovative compensation program administration to foster enhanced staff performance, productivity and commitment, as well as conformance to corporate policies.

Experience with acquisitions, down-sizing, collective bargaining relations, and arbitration, as well as contract negotiations for represented and non-represented personnel.

Consistently able to initiate and reinforce appropriate safety standards for an enriched work environment and reduced accident activity.

Interface with the President, Managing Director, Management Board Members and management in general to provide input as well as interpretation of human resource policies and programs.

Successfully reduced corporate medical costs and sick pay dispersals as well as initiated an employee recreation program for improved health and morale.

PIPING
Pipefitting Foreman

o Over 10 years responsible experience in piping for such applications as paper mills, hydrogen units, sulfur plants, pipelines, butane loading racks and sub-stations.

o Comprehensive large project expertise.

o Extensive troubleshooting and problem solving skills.

o Demonstrated ability to work with all types of alloys, from chrome and stainless steel to monell and carbon steel.

o Sound quality control and quality assurance experience.

o Seasoned scheduling and manpower planning proficiency.

o Consistently able to meet scheduled deadlines.

o Capable of monitoring and complying with OSHA standards and requirements.

o Worked as a liaison between Brown and Root and the client on a major project.

o Able to read and draw blueprints, as troubleshoot required changes upon demand.

PROCUREMENT
Buyer

Experience in purchasing with a track record for effecting high inventory turnover and minimal out of stocks.

Comprehensive ability to forecast, procure and distribute a variety of products, from general merchandise to health and beauty aids.

Extensive troubleshooting and problem solving skills utilized in expediting products to and from distribution centers.

Demonstrated ability to effectively interface with vendors, in addition to contract negotiations and competitive bids.

Expertise with special orders, in-house transfers and purchase order processing, as well as with manual and on-line ordering systems.

Seasoned inventory reporting relative to dollar, cube and in-stock conditions.

Maintain open communication with product managers regarding market needs and trends through interpersonal relations.

Experience performing daily project scheduling as well as Purchase Order follow-ups and shipment status.

Accounting competence in such areas as receivables, payables, collections, payroll and monthly statements.

Possess understanding of capital justifications and return on investment schedules.

Computer programming in addition to proficiency with Lotus, TSO, SAS, and Word to update various reports and budgets.

Informed merchandisers as to display requirements for upcoming promotions.

Dr. Lawrence Peterson

Corporate Procurement Officer

Over 8 years' experience in corporate supply materials with a track record for decreasing costs in addition to increasing operational efficiency.

Centralized purchasing proficiency supported by vendor and supplier negotiations for improved cost effectiveness.

Extensive troubleshooting and problem solving skills pertinent to technical fabric analysis and development, as well as expediting products to and from distribution centers.

Profit and Loss accountability includes projections for usage, budget and inventory control in conjunction with a plant accountability program to reduce product obsolescence.

Organized a centralized purchasing program and procurement activities throughout the national network as well as improved shipping date coordination, rate discounts and product tracking.

Ensure compliance with FMVSS-302 federal standards as well as standards affecting wearability and light fastness.

Strong supervision skills supported by hiring, training and scheduling proficiency for enhanced performance and productivity.

Conduct weekly staff meetings for improved operational integrity and coordination with organizational parameters.

Interface with Design, Marketing, management, and Divisional Directors pertinent to operational needs assessments.

Currently initiating and implementing a computer system for online communication throughout network utilizing the VAX system.

QUALITY ASSURANCE

Quality Assurance Manager

O Over 19 years involvement in production processes.
O Extensive management experience in an industrial setting.
O Scheduling and manpower planning experience.
O Hands-on production exposure.
O Statistical Process Control expertise.
O First article inspections and statistical samplings.
O Methods improvements and cost reduction abilities.
O Efficiency oriented for increased performance and productivity.
O Facilities planning and capital justification experience.
O Warranty analysis and administration.
O Heavy interface skills with production and maintenance.
O Background in metallurgy and heat treating.
O Shipping, receiving and warehousing experience.
O Bilingual - fluent in both Spanish and English.

Quality Manager

o Experience providing leadership for developing, analyzing and maintaining the Total Quality Management concept.

o Comprehensive in-house start-up expertise includes debugging all quality processes and procedures as well as establishing total documentation.

o Extensive troubleshooting and problem solving skills pertinent to quality specifications includes frequent recommendations for enhanced operational control.

o Demonstrated computer literacy with Lotus 1-2-3 is supported by proficiency with DOS for improved management reporting and compliance monitoring.

o Sound interface competence with corporate and regulatory personnel to ensure compliance with stated regulations as well as to initiate and revise quality techniques.

o Consistently able to function effectively in pressure situations to meet scheduled deadlines.

o Staff training and development abilities - act as trainer for all facility personnel regarding Total Quality Management principles.

o Can perform analytical, chemical and microbiological tests to assure the quality of finished products.

RACING
Motorcycle Racing Specialist

Over 15 years' experience riding motorcycles backed by the desire to successfully compete nationally.

Comprehensive insight into the mechanical aspects of motorcycles supported by extensive modification expertise in such areas as suspension, carburetors, exhaust and ergonomics.

Familiar with the changing needs of particular racing circumstances and desire to compete in the 750 to Open Class.

Extensive troubleshooting and analytical problem solving skills for enhanced track performance.

Demonstrated ability to finish races - have entered 3 novice races and finished 10th and 7th and subsequently 1st in the final race with improved elapsed times.

Demonstrated ability to function effectively in pressure situations.

Consistently set high performance goals with a strong emphasis on safety.

Possess excellent health habits and maintain fitness and stamina through various sports related activities.

Will also be competing in Motocross races with a Suzuki RM 250 to enhance balance, coordination and ability to respond to the unexpected.

Maintain currency with the sport.

RAILROAD
Railroad Specialist

o Over 14 years' experience in railroad operations with specialized exposure in such occupational roles as Conductor, Brakeman, Switchman, Engine Foreman, Employee in Charge and Service Attendant.

o Comprehensive safety record backed by extensive classes in hazardous materials, diesel and locomotive maintenance.

o Extensive troubleshooting and problem solving skills relative to switching and scheduling.

o Demonstrated supervision proficiency relative to engineers, switchmen and helpers.

o Experience making runs from Los Angeles to Barstow and San Diego.

o Insure that proper loading and unloading procedures are followed.

o Inform Engineer as to track bulletins and track warrants affecting train movement.

o Sound customer relations skills include experience as a Service Attendant and Employee in Charge.

o Interface with Engineers, Switchmen, and other train personnel for enhanced transportation and safety proficiency.

REAL ESTATE
Property Manager

Experience in property management backed by multiple unit operation, unit rentals, rent collections, evictions, auditing of client accounts, purchasing of supplies and bid negotiations.

Comprehensive analytical decision making abilities in conjunction with extensive troubleshooting and problem solving skills for increased operational efficiency.

Demonstrated administrative skills include budgeting, inventory control, purchasing and payroll verification.

Familiar with the current laws and regulations concerning leasing transactions.

Vendor selection experience backed by bid negotiations and contract administration.

Strong maintenance and repair proficiency for improved facility housekeeping and safety.

Sound scheduling and coordinating expertise relative to maintenance, repair services and inspections.

Seasoned accounting abilities includes payables, receivables, bank transactions and cash control management.

Consistently facilitate the efficient utilization of manpower and capital resources.

Capable of interfacing effectively with city, county, state and federal representatives as well as with individuals from diverse cultural backgrounds.

Real Estate Developer

Over 20 year's expertise in the Real Estate industry.

Comprehensive experience in strategic planning, marketing

analysis, and economic feasibility studies, including site selection, finance, credit, purchasing and closing.

Extensive expertise in appraisals, negotiation of leases, contracts and purchase agreements.

Maintain extended contact with brokers, appraisers, attorneys, architects, engineers, as well as contractors, lenders developers and title companies for effective networking.

Strong track record for project profitability and functionality.

Proven site acquisition techniques and guidelines.

Able to maintain the highest per unit volume average with the greatest return on invested capital.

Conceptualized, staffed and implemented a previously non-existent Real Estate Division for the Western United States.

Demonstrated effectiveness with governmental bodies such as planning commissions, city councils, boards of appeal and environmental groups.

Extensive troubleshooting and problem solving abilities.

Creative marketing for enhanced project development and increased profitability.

Experience in the establishment and administration of policies for enhanced organizational efficiency.

Extensive supervision experience relative to personnel, projects, materials and equipment.

Significant track record in personal sales and closing. Proficient with advertising coordination and organization.

Real Estate Appraiser

Experienced with FHA, VA, and Conventional Appraisals, including policy guidelines for single family residential properties.

Knowledge of Real Estate principles and practices to assure conformity with regulations as well as to enhance client satisfaction.

Excellent research skills pertinent to market analyses to accurately determine market values for single family residential properties.

Proficient with site analysis in conjunction with legal considerations, zoning restrictions, encumbrances and easements.

Competent at identifying adverse property and construction features that impact on the marketability of respective properties and locations.

Accurate neighborhood assessments which address such environmental and demographic concerns as noise, population, traffic and accessibility to local services.

Consistently able to provide fast project turnarounds to meet tight schedule restraints.

Analytical decision making abilities backed by strategic troubleshooting and problem solving proficiency.

Demonstrated ability to work independently or as part of a team in high pressure settings.

Well-developed oral and written communication skills backed by excellent telecommunications proficiency as well as stand-up presentation competence.

Title Survey Analyst

o Over 13 years responsible experience in the title insurance industry.

o Comprehensive management, supervision, and administration abilities.

o Extensive troubleshooting and problem solving skills for staff recommendations relative to potential risk significance.

o Expertise in generating monthly reports for supervisors and department heads relative to work submitted by their personnel.

o Sound understanding of basic, intermediate, and advanced legal descriptions, escrow, conveyances, trust deeds, liens, performance appraisals, and Gordon Wattles legal descriptions.

o Seasoned drafting and hands-on board skills, relative to modifications of existing maps either recorded tract or parcel maps or assessors maps for lay persons unfamiliar with technical title terminology.

o Excellent interpersonal skills for enhanced customer relations have received letters of appreciation from clients.

o Capable of performing field inspections on property to verify information collected in the title search.

o Ability to read blueprints and plot plans.

o Proficiency with composing legal descriptions from survey data or maps as well as draw maps from legal descriptions.

o Capable of determining the sufficiency of supplied legal descriptions.

o Perform mathematical traverses and closures to locate potential gaps and overlaps.

RESEARCH AND DEVELOPMENT
Research and Development Specialist

Comprehensive research and development skills with emphasis on operational efficiency and cost reduction.

Able to design as well as work from conceptual designs to create prototypes assemblies.

Extensive troubleshooting and problem solving skills relative to the manufacture of specialized parts and components, including the analysis of malfunctions.

Make recommendations for material substitutions and manpower capabilities relative to manufacturing feasibility.

Initiate and apply new methods and procedures to successfully test opto-mechanical devices.

Possess experience working with a variety of materials, including plastics, wood, metal, and glass.

Capable of reading blueprints and wiring schematics as well as diagnosing systems performance.

Laser optics expertise includes alignments, installations, multi-lense configurations and cleanings.

Lab setting experience includes capital justifications.

Extensive machine shop proficiency includes such equipment as lathes, mills, and grinders.

Test equipment includes interferometers, oscilloscopes, and multimeters.

Experience working in microelectronics as well as sophisticated electromechanical devices.

Interface proficiency with Engineering, Purchasing, Manufacturing, Tooling, Maintenance, and Vendors.

Research and Development - Food

Experience analyzing food products with regard to fat, moisture, ash, protein and dietary fibers for enhanced quality control and customer satisfaction.

Comprehensive research skills include biochemical investigations and statistical documentation to complement as well as further research and development initiatives.

Extensive troubleshooting and problem solving skills pertinent to sensory studies applicable to new and existing products.

Experience with menu analysis and development for enhanced sales and promotional response.

Background in processing and presentation ranges from organ meats to pastry products.

Demonstrated interpersonal relations proficiency for enhanced rapport and cooperation with clients and co-workers.

Interface with vendors, Food Technologists, production and marketing personnel to enhance the quality and integrity of food products.

Sound organization and prioritization skills for improved operational efficiency.

Seasoned experience with food processing and presentation for improved client response.

Strong attention to detail backed by extensive analytical decision making abilities.

Capable of working well independently or as a productive team member.

Computer literacy includes Microsoft Word, Microsoft

Works. Excell and DAC Easy.

RESTAURANT
Culinary Specialist

Over 9 years' experience in the preparation and presentation of culinary food products backed by attention to dietary concerns.

Management supervision for enhanced business, menu and staff development.

Extensive troubleshooting and problem solving skills for the quick diagnosis and remedy of operational dysfunctions.

Demonstrated analytical decision making abilities supported by budgeting, forecasting and projecting proficiency.

Attention to detail results in enhanced quality control and improved customer relations.

Numerous awards and certifications ranging from artistic centerpieces to the presentation of crustaceans.

Capable of expediting food service sanitation and hygiene for safety and improved working conditions.

Familiar with a variety of dining formats, from fast food to institutional settings, as well as intimate dining.

Interface with customers from various cultures and backgrounds for enhanced rapport and repeat business.

Expedite promotional catering functions encompassing ranging from informal gatherings to large banquets.

Restaurant Manager

o Several years progressive experience in supervising food preparation for American and European cuisine.

o Extensive troubleshooting and problem solving skills includes five star restaurant exposure and start-up expertise to diagnose service dysfunctions as well as initiate remedies for enhanced revenue and customer satisfaction.

o Supervision competence encompasses scheduling and manpower planning to maximize human and capital resources.

o Familiar with the challenging requirements of a full service dining establishment, including banquet and room service activities. Interface with clients from diverse cultural backgrounds for enhanced rapport and cooperation.

o Demonstrated ability to perform food costing, inventory control, and specialty item purchasing.

o Organization and prioritization expertise to facilitate increased levels of operational efficiency.

o Sound interface skills with health officials to conform to stated regulations.

o Seasoned staff development proficiency pertinent to training and development with particular emphasis on service, safety and commitment.

o Consistently able to function effectively in pressure environments to manage large banquet crowds as well as daily, high volume eating requirements.

o Capable of managing total food preparation, including soups, hors d'oeuvres and international specialty items.

o Familiar with ice carvings and other forms of food merchandising for enhanced customer satisfaction.

Dr. Lawrence Peterson

Restaurant Manager

Over 20 years diversified restaurant experience backed by multiple unit management proficiency to maximize human and capital resources.

Profit and Loss responsibility includes budgeting, sales forecasting, purchasing, inventory and expense control with a track record for enhancing sales and profits.

Extensive troubleshooting and problem solving skills applicable to all organizational areas to anticipate, diagnose and remedy operational dysfunctions.

New and existing facilities development includes site selections, construction, interior design, capital equipment justifications and vendor contract negotiations.

Demonstrated marketing expertise pertinent to demographic penetration, advertising, food, beverage and entertainment promotions, as well as media experience with radio and newspaper coverage.

Sound business turnaround proficiency includes staff reorganizations, policy and procedure initiation, strategic trainings, and management meetings to foster compliance with corporate objectives.

Seasoned interface skills with Alcohol and Beverage Control, the Health Department, Police and Fire Departments, OSHA and such internal departments as Legal to minimize insurance liability.

Capable of providing recommendations to senior management, district managers, general managers and affiliated personnel to foster enhanced sales, quality and customer satisfaction.

Strategic leadership abilities include critical staff training and development for increased performance, productivity and commitment.

RETAIL
Retail Administrative Support Analyst

Over 10 years' experience in retail business operations with a track record for assisting in the enhancement of store performance and productivity.

Customer service proficiency includes troubleshooting and problem solving skills with regard to credit authorization and follow-up.

Interface with management and other department personnel for improved operational efficiency.
Analyze productivity, ordering, price changes, billing and telephone utilization reports.

Assist with grand openings and train personnel in the use of NCR and IBM system operation, updating manuals when applicable.

Frequently track store programs for management feedback and response.

Ad coordination experience backed by the ability to assume positions of responsibility.

Familiar with Unix, Word, and LOTUS 1-2-3.

Well-developed oral and written communication skills supported by Spanish fluency to interface with individuals from diverse cultural backgrounds.

Can fulfill a variety of challenging assignments through effective decision making in pressure situations.

Able to adapt quickly to new organizational settings, facilitating a team atmosphere and enhancing customer satisfaction.

Dr. Lawrence Peterson

Retail Manager

Staff training and development skills have resulted in the highest level of management personnel in chain, as well as the lowest turnover of staff personnel.

Strategic scheduling of 40-80 personnel staff has resulted in very high return on payroll dollars invested.

Outstanding record of profit, loss, and expense control.

High inventory turnover statistics and control.

Experienced with store remodeling's and installations.

Competent in strategic merchandising which takes advantage of consumer buying patterns for augmented sales and profits.

Adept with local advertising and in-store promotions, as well as strategic market and demographic analysis.

Utilize the fundamentals of time-management for increased operational efficiency.

Retail Specialist

Extensive knowledge of China, China related products and clothing, to include fashion merchandising.

Strategic product development expertise geared to local demographics.

Demonstrated troubleshooting and problem solving skills.

Major remodeling experience relative to home entertaining. Implemented - directed a successful bridal consulting program.

Comprehensive supervisory expertise in a retail setting. Have trained and developed 4 management trainees.

Sound inventory decision making - to include shrinkage control. Seasoned customer relations abilities for enhanced sales.

Consistency meets sales objectives.

Capable of assuming greater responsibility in buying or sales.

Scheduling and computerized business analysis expertise.

Interface with buyers for effective inventory representation. Facilitate sales through forecasts and staff quotas.

SALES
Air Conditioning Sales

Sales and marketing proficiency supported by a strong management skills.

Administrative abilities include budgeting, forecasting, and projections, as well as purchasing, inventory, cost control, payroll, and bookkeeping expertise.

Accomplished customer product sales include Carrier, Payne, Day & Night, Trane, York, Rheem, and Honeywell.

Capable of servicing a large number of accounts and representing multiple product lines.

Demonstrated ability to launch new products, open new accounts, and service existing accounts.

Experienced with needs assessments backed by an understanding of consumer behavior and buyer motivation.

Comprehensive knowledge of demographics and strategic advertising for increased market penetration.

Extensive troubleshooting and problem solving skills for the quick diagnosis and remedy of account issues.

Possess stand up presentation skills for product development and organizational efficiency.

Dr. Lawrence Peterson

Electrical Sales

Over 16 year's progressive management experience with a proven track record for enhancing operational and account efficiency.

Comprehensive administrative activities include profit and loss accountability, budgeting, forecasting, and projecting for enhanced fiscal control and organizational performance.

Extensive account troubleshooting and problem solving proficiency allows for the application of strategic recommendations to organizational dysfunctions.

Demonstrated analytical decision making abilities from both a marketing and technical perspective result in the maximization of profit endeavors.

Proficient in market data analysis and demographics as well as competition product lines for increased market penetration and account revenue.

Marketing and organizational competence allows for the servicing of multiple accounts as well as diverse product lines in different project stages.

Interpersonal communication skills for improved product presentations to key decision makers as well as to foster leads from trade show demonstrations.

Sound facilities layout and merchandising proficiency for greater product visibility, mix, display impact and turnover.

Facilitate advertising and in-store promotional endeavors to promote traffic, volume, and profitability.

Able to perform master scheduling and manpower planning activities to maximize capital and human resources.

Personnel skills include hiring, evaluating, training, scheduling and manpower planning for effective coverage as well as staff development.

Wood Product Sales

Over 20 years successful sales experience backed by sales management proficiency.
Profit and loss responsibility is supported by sound administrative abilities.

Extensive sales experience includes light to medium duty trucks, new and used cars, and fleet contracts.

Initiated a successful truck fleet department for a leading dealership with significant profit results.

Experience initiating state and municipality bids and proposals.

Extensive involvement with ordering and inventory control.

Telemarketing and sales promotional activities have consistently resulted in significant account development.

Interpersonal skills with customers, other dealers, brokers, and credit union personnel for enhanced rapport.

Staff training and development proficiency has resulted in effective team building and account development.

Currently Vice President and former President of the Dodge-Plymouth-Jeep Fleet Managers' Guild.

Dr. Lawrence Peterson

Pharmaceutical Representative

Can open new accounts, service existing accounts, open new territories and. launch new pharmaceutical brands.

Proficient with market data analysis and demographics to identify potential product applications as well as increase market penetration.

Extensive troubleshooting and problem solving skills for the quick diagnosis and remedy of customer service issues.

Capable of servicing a large number of accounts and representing multiple product categories.

Sound knowledge of medications supported by experience assisting physicians with patient care.

Seasoned analytical skills backed by basic accounting and administration abilities.

Excellent grasp of human behavior and buyer motivation in addition to an understanding of science for insight into pharmaceutical applications.

Capable of interfacing with physicians, nurses, purchasing agents, hospital personnel and HMO representatives for additional account revenue.

Well-developed oral and written communication skills backed by the ability to effectively relate with individuals from diverse cultural backgrounds.

Cabinet Sales

Several years' responsible experience as a successful Factory Representative marketing kitchen and bathroom cabinetry.

Comprehensive understanding of finished wood products, including flooring and cabinets.

Extensive troubleshooting and problem solving skills for the rapid resolution of account issues.

Demonstrated ability to open new accounts, service existing accounts, open new territories and launch new brands.

Seasoned background providing bids for new construction accounts.

Opened credit limits and corrected credit dysfunctions while preserving customer relations.

Consistently recognized for outstanding sales performance.

Capable of servicing a large number of accounts as well as multiple product lines.

Have initiated a successful dealer network in California with significant sales growth.

Interface with key decision makers to generate new account revenue.

Experience making stand up presentations in both technical and nontechnical areas for dealer development.

Dealer support activities include product design, merchandising, inventory control and promotional sales techniques.

Previous experience as a Contract Sales Representative for industrial accounts.

SECURITY
Retail Security

Over 15 years' experience in the security field, 14 of which being in security supervision.

Demonstrated ability to formulate and implement security policies and procedures for successful loss prevention.

Staff training and development abilities relative to security personnel for enhance organizational efficiency.

Competent at recognizing security deficiencies and developing appropriate solutions to minimize vulnerability.

Manpower planning skills for economical security coverage.

Experienced with security reporting and documentation.

Security budget formulation, to include forecasting.

Extensive experience with computer security investigations.

Close circuit television surveillance expertise.

Experience determining security violations through chemical analysis.

Over a 95% conviction rate for security violations.

K-9 dog deployment and handling - Shepard and Rottweiler.

Interface with all levels of management, including security presentations to upper management.

Have worked in close conjunction with local law enforcement officials relative to security assignments.

Extensive retail operations and warehouse expertise.

WAREHOUSING
Dispatcher

o Over 10 years responsible experience in Dispatching with a track record for improving staff performance, productivity and commitment.

o Comprehensive analytical skills include project tracking and prioritization abilities to coordinate a variety of on-going assignments simultaneously.

o Extensive troubleshooting and problem solving skills to correct operational problems as well as to provide recommendations for implementation.

o Demonstrated ability to dispatch vehicles and technicians to provide for efficient maintenance, service, repair and customer satisfaction.

o Interpersonal skills include interface with individuals from diverse cultural backgrounds for improved team dynamics and customer relations.

o Consistently able to meet scheduled deadlines through leadership and analytical decision making abilities.

o Computer literate to maximize data processing initiatives.

o Personnel skills include scheduling and manpower planning, in addition to staff training and development abilities to maximize human resources.

Distribution Manager

Responsible experience in distribution backed by a track record for improving operational efficiency as well as maximizing human and capital resources.

Comprehensive troubleshooting and problem solving skills to rapidly diagnose and remedy operational dysfunctions.

Demonstrated ability to initiate effective policies and procedures for improved quality control, distribution and order accuracy.

Sound analytical decision making proficiency for improved Profit and Loss accountability - can work effectively within strict budgetary guidelines.

Seasoned start-up expertise includes facilities layout, equipment acquisition, staff hiring and training with emphasis on safety and organizational coordination.

Expertise with inventory and production control - initiated a scrap recovery program to minimize costs and maximize revenue.

Consistently able to function effectively in pressure situations to meet scheduled deadlines.

Capable of performing scheduling and manpower planning endeavors as well as prioritizing and expediting accurate orders.

Have been recognized for exceeding high-volume records for product shipments for volume levels exceeding 800,000 units per week.

Interface with management, production and finance personnel in addition to company owners to facilitate organizational objectives.

WRITING
Service Writer

Over 20 years' experience in business operations with a track record for improving operational performance.

Comprehensive troubleshooting and problem solving skills applicable to the challenging demands of service writing.

Demonstrated understanding of automotive specifications and systems for expedient diagnosis and repair.

Sound selling proficiency to identify and recommend appropriate maintenance and aftermarket products.

Seasoned experience with blueprint reading and specifications can be applied to wiring schematics and new car configurations.

Consistently able to promote customer satisfaction through strategic interpersonal communication skills.

Capable of assuming positions of greater responsibility.

Can function effectively in pressure environments to meet scheduled deadlines.

Able to interface with customers, the service department, and management for improved operational efficiency.

Strong attention to detail is readily applied to vehicle inspections.

Dr. Lawrence Peterson

Sports Writer

Over 20 years' experience as a sports writer and copy editor.

Sports page layout ability includes section fronts and agate pages.

Ability to compose creative headlines.

Experience in editing wire and locally produced copy.

Wide exposure in sports with competence in covering football, basketball, baseball, auto racing, track and field, as well as golf and tennis.

Cover sporting events from several perspectives (sidebar features, general event coverage).

Compose feature stories on sports.

Write weekly column emphasizing radio and television events and personalities.

Strong photography skills (action shots in sporting events).

Demonstrated computer skills for processing and page assignments.

Excellent telecommunication skills for gathering, organizing and interpreting incoming news information.

Effective use of public relations for enhanced news input.

Outstanding proofreading, punctuation and grammar skills.

Function well under pressure to meet scheduled deadlines.

Proven staff training and development abilities relative to sports interns.

CHAPTER FIVE

EXECUTIVE SUMMARIES THAT WORK

COVER LETTERS

Effective resumes are strategic marketing presentations. Persuasive cover letters approach the busy decision maker with the bottom line. The name and address on the envelope is sufficient to get the document to the decision maker. The cover letter starts by promising a benefit. Effective cover letters are Executive Summaries reinforcing the Objective, if used, and Summary of Qualifications. For impact, the closing line asks for an interview so benefits can be discussed in greater detail. Cover letters consist of three parts: the Introduction, Body, and the Conclusion encompassing a call to action.

Effective introductions can begin with a simple thank you. For example, "Thank you for the opportunity to present an outline of my background and qualifications." By using the word "outline," it is suggested there are more benefits coming at the time of the interview. The next step is the introduction restating the objective for parallel construction with the resume.

Introduction:
Seasoned sales specialist presently seeking affiliation with a challenging wholesale firm to apply my diverse marketing background to new account generation.

Alternative:

Sales specialist demonstrating ten years of progressive success in marketing supported by seasoned account management proficiency.

The summary of qualifications was created prior to the Cover Letter and follows next.

General SOQ data in marketing:

o Over ten years progressive experience in marketing supported by seasoned account management proficiency.

o Experience initiating account transactions, servicing existing accounts, opening new territories and launching specialized products.

o Commercial building products familiarity ranging from doors to roofing materials.

o Extensive problem solving expertise applied to the identification and remedy of account deficiencies for enhanced customer retention and repeat sales.

o Experience performing client needs assessments so as to effectively present the most marketable aspects of a given product or service.

o Demographic proficiency includes expertise with economic trend indicators as well as client profile analyses for improved market penetration.

o Advertising competence includes exposure to diverse media sources, from television and radio, to newspapers and technical trade journals.

o Seasoned interpersonal communication skills include stand-up presentations to key decision makers in addition to trade show promotions to leverage leads into viable accounts.

How the summary is converted into a Cover Letter

Thank you for the opportunity to present an outline of my background. A summary of my qualifications includes over ten years progressive experience in marketing firmly supported by seasoned account management proficiency. I can readily initiate client transactions, open new territories and launch specialized products. My familiarity with commercial building products ranges from doors to roofing materials with expertise in customer retention and repeat sales.

My experience with economic trend indicators and client profile analyses has resulted in improved market penetration. Further, my advertising competence encompasses all media sources, from television and radio, to newspapers and technical trade journals. Finally, my communication skills include stand-up presentations to key decision makers as well as trade show promotions to leverage leads into viable accounts.

An interview will allow me to discuss in greater detail how my background and experience can readily assist you in accomplishing your account objectives.

FOLLOW-UP

Nothing convinces a procrastinating employer like a follow-up note that reinforces interest in the position. Post cards are excellent "Thank You" notes. An effective enclosure might state, "Look forward to applying my skills and abilities to the benefit of your organization." A hand-written note is effective because of its personal nature. If a formal letter is called for, include a thank you along with benefits to the company prior to closing with a positive statement. Keep follow-ups brief and focused.

I wanted to drop you a short note thanking you once again for the opportunity to present my background and qualifications. I look forward to applying my skills and abilities to the benefit of your organization. Feel free to contact me at your earliest convenience.

Creating a List of Skills and Abilities

Effective resumes are founded upon accurate assessments of past experience, potential and abilities. Begin with an outline of education, affiliations, licenses and certificates. Job history precedes the Summary of Qualifications because background automatically indicates what can be connected to the objective. Even the weakest background can be transformed into an effective resume by using a series of persuasive selling points.

For example, "Am capable of initiating new accounts," implies an ability not actual experience. The next step is to look into your background for skills and abilities supporting such a belief. With each job description ask, "What accomplishments or special projects have I worked on?" When your background is lean, look to other areas for additional support; particularly classes or school projects which bolster expertise. Begin by creating an outline called a decision tree. Such a process serves to elicit additional questions needing to be asked to ensure the subject has been adequately covered. A typical Manager's decision tree might take the following approach:

Title: Plant Manager
Product or Service: Trucks.
Supervise people?
How many people?
Kinds of people?
How many shifts?
Supervise projects?
Kinds of projects?
Dollar amount of projects?
Kinds of departments?

Resume Application

Plant Manager for major truck manufacturing plant employing over 900 employees in three production shifts to produce 27 custom units per day. Routinely implement a $113 million dollar operating budget encompassing both assembly line and support personnel. In addition to developing numerous special project initiatives, have successfully executed a plant renovation to improve production processes and minimize off-line repairs. Project management included capital justifications, equipment procurement and subcontractor coordination to meet scheduled timelines.

People and projects require scheduling. What programs do you use? Do you perform master scheduling? Do you set a manufacturing backlog? Do you perform manpower or capacity planning? Do you use statistical controls? Do you perform routing or flow charting?

Resume Application

Routinely set a $2 million dollar manufacturing backlog using Schedule software. Also utilize Gantt charts to facilitate master scheduling, manpower planning, capacity and routing strategies to maximize capital and human resources.

People Skills

Recruit other employees?Interview other employees? Make hiring decisions?Perform personnel evaluations? Handle labor disputes?Train others? Write policies or procedures? Leadership skills?

Resume Application

Personnel skills include recruiting, interviewing and hiring recommendations regarding potential professional openings within the corporate structure. Conducted training orientation programs for new hires. Successfully prevented a major plant shut down through strategic negotiation with collective bargaining representatives. Provided critical leadership in complement of a plant reorganization by initiating numerous modification orders and field policies.

Financial Skills

Profit and loss responsibility? Initiate bid proposals? Budgeting, forecasting, projecting? Discharge estimating duties? Do you initiate bid proposals? Cost reduction experience?

Resume Application

Operational responsibility includes profit and loss accountability supported by budgeting, forecasting and projecting proficiency. Direct the initiation of realistic estimates and bid proposals in compliance with proposed contract guidelines with particular attention given to make or buy decisions that reduce costs.

Sales and Marketing Skills

Open new accounts? Service existing accounts? Open new territories? Launch new brands? Advertising or promotions? Merchandise products? Research and development? Specialized products?

Resume Application

Marketing expertise includes the ability to foster new account generation, service existing transactions, open new territories and launch specialized products and services. Background in advertising and merchandising has successfully resulted in the significant development of additional account revenue due to the application of analytical research skills in conjunction with seasoned forecasting proficiency.

Administrative Skills

Perform contract administration? Monitor regulatory conformance? Involved in data processing? Certify or document processes?

Resume Application

Utilized a 360 Mainframe computer to track and document deviations from specified contract specifications for enhanced conformance to program objectives as well as regulatory mandates.

Interface Skills

Interface with clients? International relations exposure? Interact with institutions? Proficient with languages?

Resume Application

Interface with clients, key decision makers and affiliated, in-house program personnel for improved response to project directives. Fluency in English and German allows for improved communication with Bonn headquarters to respond to client requests from the United States.

Obviously, there are many other skills and abilities that can be highlighted. Computer skills include hardware and software configurations as well as language programming.

GROUPING LIKE ITEMS

Resumes display a four step writing process: Organization, Prioritization, Simplification, and Stylization.

Organization: Like items are linked together to facilitate comprehension. Management differs from Administration, which is dissimilar to Personnel. Shipping is different than purchasing, which is separate from warehousing. In contrast, Profit and Loss accountability is similar to budgeting, forecasting, projecting and cash flow management. Like items are sequentially grouped with the most important item listed first. Dissimilar items are arranged by level of importance as well as congruity with other data.

Prioritization: A Manager may be responsible for a wide range of Administrative and Personnel duties. These activities follow a primary duty, that of managing human and capital resources. Supervision precedes budgeting, and fiscal control precedes hiring. All three activities are important. Priority is critical to create a favorable impression. If the employer stops reading they may still make a hiring decision based on critical skills.

Simplification: Resumes eliminate unnecessary details while highlighting important considerations. Instead of listing all geographical areas within a Sales Manager's domain, it suffices to write national and international account responsibility. In place of enumerating the total number of companies a Sales Manager represents, it is effective to list the classification of companies i.e., manufacturing, construction, and service. Avoid belaboring the obvious.

Stylization: Effective writing is less obvious than poor journalism but certainly more apparent. When a resume is well-conceived the words disappear behind the apparent meaning. Poorly written documents confuse and annoy employers with unnecessary redundancy and distractions. Effective resumes are persuasive and elegant. As a general rule, the more pertinent and focused the information in the resume; the stronger and more persuasive the communication. As Edgar Allen Poe once said, "I wish I had the time to write you a short letter." Filling pages with verbosity makes for a poor presentation; it takes skill to condense a lifetime of information into a comprehensible format. One page documents are excellent for candidates making less than $30,000 per annum. Higher paying positions generally necessitate more than a thumb nail sketch of background to motivate employee interest.

CHAPTER SIX

ACHIEVING JOB SATISFACTION

CHOOSING A CAREER OBJECTIVE

Homework is the cure to overcoming career problems. The library has several publications on career development. The Occupational Outlook Handbook describes a wide variety of positions, along with academic requirements, range of compensation, and future growth potential. If moving to another state, the Places Rated Almanac is also a valuable resource because it provides information about potential jobs, housing, recreation, educational resources, the average per capita income, medical facilities, the weather, and even the transportation situation.
The more information we have about a specific opportunity, the better we can effectively evaluate it. If transportation is a concern, working in Los Angeles is out of the question. If specialized medical treatment is required, the location of hospitals and medical services is critical to a career decision requiring relocation to a rural area.

If a specific career objective cannot be identified, a "generic" resume is created that puts forth our most attractive skills and abilities. The down side of the generic approach is it lacks teeth because it forces the employer to make the necessary connections.

Generic example:

Business Specialist seeks increased responsibility in a challenging environment where background and experience can be applied to the efficient satisfaction of organizational objectives.

Such a presentation allows the employer to read in virtually anything. The disadvantage has to do with employment history. Employers tend to assume we will be most effective if we "stick to the knitting," meaning the decision to grant us an interview is based on matching our background with potential openings. If we previously rode shotgun on an ice cream truck and now want to practice our formidable marketing expertise within the context of a different career objective, what probable decision would the employer likely conclude? "Has extensive knowledge of 50 different kinds of ice cream," though impressive, doesn't translate well, does it?

Although career assistance can be a valuable asset, responsibility for choosing a particular field or position within a given area resides with the job seeker. If we do not choose the objective of our own free will, we will almost certainly not be committed to it regardless of how much sense it makes or potential compensation it promises. Be careful in asking friends, associates and counselors for direction. Have you ever met anyone who took a test, followed its directions, and achieved occupational bliss?

The first question to ask is, "WHAT TYPE OF POSITION AM I LOOKING FOR?" Most of us select a position similar to the one we most recently occupied, or a higher position within the same field because it takes advantage of what we already know. Focusing on realistic probabilities within the context of our skills, experience, and aspirations is productive, but does require knowing something about the various positions afforded in the market place. Modern job seekers look at work as an assignment instead of a life-long commitment.

If recently terminated, laid off or forced out, distance may be desired from the disagreeable incident. But "throwing the baby out with the bathwater," may not be a wise career move. Therefore, total honesty is needed in delineating between the incident and the career field. Was it the company, the job, a particular boss, or a personality problem causing the incident? Harboring resentment may undermine an excellent resume with a defensive interview. No one likes bad news.

Positions that challenge creativity are strongly encouraged. Taking the first job that comes along without realizing the long range ramifications of an impulsive act is a tragic waste of human potential. Why waste precious time, energy and money on perfunctory positions encouraging brain death? Impulsive acts are like signing a high interest loan without thought as to the actual cost in years to come. The expense of being underutilized is more than financial because self-esteem and mental health are at stake.

One of the greatest obstacles to occupational fulfillment is hopelessness. Problems with work encourage a slump, downcast eyes, self-pity, and difficulty expressing valuable experience because faith is lost. The first step in regaining confidence is to create a marketing document which effectively portrays skills and abilities as potential company benefits.

RESUME WRITING QUESTIONS AND ANSWERS

HANDLING PROBLEMS AND EXCEPTIONS IN THE RESUME

QUESTION: What if my work experience is incompatible with the job I am going for?

ANSWER: There are several ways of responding to this question. We can emphasize a SOQ full of promises while minimizing our actual experience. We can rearrange our work experience so that it reflects the best fit for the next job we are going for. Obviously, omitting the dates creates a more convincing scenario. Care should be taken to ensure that the proper tense is used. If no longer working for the company, past tense is correct. Our past can be reinterpreted by changing the titles of job descriptions to match more closely the sought for opening. If the position calls for a supervisor and previous experience was as a manager, a little poetic liberty will harm no one.

QUESTION: How do I handle my lack of education?

ANSWER: If a document is properly conceived and arranged with a list of valuable benefits to an organization, education is often beside the point. Means for bolstering education include listing pertinent life or instructional experiences which demonstrate competence, even though a degree is not present. Enrollment in a degree program carries weight, even though we have not attended the first class.

QUESTION: Do I need a Cover Letter for a face-to-face interview?

ANSWER: Effective cover letters serve as Executive Summaries and can both introduce the resume if mailed or handed to a potential employer in person. Even if separated the cover letter should offer sufficient benefits to elicit an offer.

QUESTION: Should I include my waitressing experience on my management resume?

ANSWER: Although total honesty is laudable, disclosing incompatible work information can potentially reduce the impact of our presentation.

QUESTION: Should I include references with my resume?

ANSWER: To ensure appetite, companies should ask for something? References are typically supplied after reciprocal interest has been established.

QUESTION: What if the ad asks for Salary History?

ANSWER: Salary histories are used to screen out candidates looking for a progressive wage. Answer ads asking for Salary History last since it is generally understood such companies are either financially burdened or stingy.

QUESTION: Will employers read more than a one-page resume?

ANSWER: Employers will continue to read as long as what they read is pertinent and promises a personal benefit. One-page documents are no longer sufficient to convince employers they should call you ahead of other candidates. Since a resume is an occupational brochure, quality of information is more important than length.

QUESTION: What about including school awards, honors, alumni societies and organizations?

ANSWER: Including honor standing at graduation is effective, but school clubs and alumni affiliation is generally not as important as actual work experience or specialized knowledge. Features are not as effective as benefits.

QUESTION: If I lack college should I include my High School?

ANSWER: High School is generally taken for granted and is not usually highlighted unless you are going for an entry level position. Rather, list pertinent workshops attended or any classes taken in college.

QUESTION: Do I need a different resume for each position sought?

ANSWER: The more pertinent the resume, the better the hook. The ideal situation would be to have your resume in a file and modify it each time you respond to a new position. Although management is management, going for management and sales requires strategic writing.

QUESTION: How specific should my resume be?

ANSWER: Reader involvement suggests the more general the skill, the more applicable to most situations. If the sought position is very specialized, then technical skills would take precedence over generic abilities.

QUESTION: Do I need a new resume when I change addresses?

ANSWER: Fortunately, computers with printers makes keeping a resume current quite easy.

QUESTION: How is the sequence of pages collated for handing in to an employer?

ANSWER: The Cover Sheet includes your name and sometimes the objective. The Cover Letter is included next and is followed by the Summary Page and Work Experience. Anything else follows last.

QUESTION: Do I paper clip or staple my pages together?

ANSWER: Never mutilate your resume. Simply bind the pages in a notebook or include them loose in a manila envelope in the proper sequence.

CHAPTER SEVEN

PUTTING IT ALL TOGETHER

Examples of Completed Resumes

ROBERT WILLIAMS
1117 Border Street
Upland, CA 91786
(714) 949-1682

Thank you for the opportunity to present an outline of my background and experience. I am a seasoned manager with sales and marketing expertise seeking increased responsibility in a challenging educational environment.

A summary of my qualifications includes over 10 years responsible experience in administration supported by sales and marketing expertise. My administrative experience includes maintaining a $4 million dollar financial aid budget, effectively managing a $900,000 departmental budget, and successfully negotiating contracts with outside vendors and service organizations. I possess troubleshooting skills for quick diagnosis and remedy of account issues. My personnel skills include hiring, training, and staff development.

I can readily open new accounts, launch new brands, and service multiple product lines. My knowledge of consumer behavior allows insight into buyer motivation for effective client needs assessments. Finally, my well-developed communication skills allow for effective interface with key decision makers.

An interview will allow me to discuss in greater detail how my background and experience, as well as my ability to adapt quickly to new settings, can assist you in accomplishing your academic objectives.

Sincerely,

Robert Williams

Dr. Lawrence Peterson

ROBERT WILLIAMS
1117 Border Street
Upland, CA 91786
(714) 949-1682

Education management and marketing specialist.

Summary of Qualifications

o Over 10 years responsible experience in administration supported by strong sales and marketing proficiency in an educational setting.

o Administrative experience includes maintaining a $4 mil-
lion dollar financial aid budget, effectively managing a
$900,000 departmental budget, and successfully negotiating
contracts with outside vendors and service organizations to
procure equipment and supplies.

o Sound troubleshooting and problem solving skills for the
quick diagnosis and remedy of account and organizational
issues, resulting in enhanced client satisfaction, repeat business and referrals.

o Personnel skills include hiring, training, staff development
and performance appraisals in addition to policies and procedures initiation and training manual development to increase new employee adaptation and efficiency.

o Consistently able to plan, implement, and monitor short
and long range marketing strategies is supported by extensive
public relations proficiency resulting for enhanced account
development.

o Capable of servicing a large number of accounts and representing multiple product lines is bolstered with market
data analysis, demographics and psychographics for increased
market penetration.

o Outstanding customer relations skills in a competitive environment includes sound knowledge of consumer behavior and buyer motivation, resulting in effective client needs assessments that identify potential marketing strategies.

o Interpersonal relations abilities for enhanced rapport and cooperation with clients and co-workers from varied cultural backgrounds.

Education

CALIFORNIA STATE UNIVERSITY - SAN BERNARDINO
Master of Arts Degree in Education.

CHAFFEY COMMUNITY COLLEGE
Associate of Arts Degree in Communication.

ROBERT WILLIAMS

Professional Experience

GOTTER UNIVERSITY, Los Angeles, CA

Director of Admissions reporting directly to the President. Responsibilities include extensive public relations and marketing activities for the recruitment of new students. Conceive and coordinate special events while planning, implementing, and monitoring short and long range marketing strategies. Set up various department telemarketing programs resulting in a 16% increase over marketing goals, as well as a substantial increase over prior year's revenue. Maintain a $4 million dollar financial aid budget which includes awarding financial aid to students representing 20 states and 30 countries. Manage a $900,000 departmental budget in conjunction with financial policy setting and vendor negotiations to procure necessary equipment and supplies.

Personnel duties involve hiring, training, and supervising a staff of professional and clerical workers, as well as conducting employee evaluations and promotion reviews. Routinely initiate policies and procedures and coordinate production of all admissions publications, including a 150 page training manual to foster new employee adaptation. Interview and counsel students with their academic, career and financial planning needs. Function as a member on the President's Cabinet and have participated as a voting member of several statewide and national professional organizations.

SAINT LUCY'S UNIVERSITY, Redding, CA

Associate Dean of Admissions responsible for hiring, training, and supervising 10 professionals who traveled extensively to interface with guidance counselors, parents and student groups. Assigned territories and monitored quotas while planning marketing strategies to increase territory performance. Devised an effective enrollment management scheme, facilitated the training and development of new admissions representatives, and maintained responsibility for recruitment and admission of foreign students.

Previously functioned as the Assistant Dean of Admissions with recruitment and marketing responsibilities throughout the United States.

Affiliations

Inland Consort for Articulation and Transfer.
National Association of Foreign Student Advisors.
Western Association of College Admissions Counselors.
National Association of College Admissions Counselors.
Pacific Associations of College Registers and Admissions Officers.

Dr. Lawrence Peterson

JOHN WORK
1150 Dancer Drive
Upland, CA 91786
(714) 949-1000

Thank you for the opportunity to present an outline of my background and qualifications. I am a professional manager with extensive international sales, purchasing and manufacturing experience.

A summary of my qualifications includes over 20 years operational expertise in such areas as profit and loss accountability, budgeting, forecasting and projecting for enhanced fiscal control. I can readily open new accounts, service existing transactions, open new territories and launch new brands. I also exhibit supervisory experience for effective scheduling, manpower planning, policy initiation and staff evaluations. My international exposure allows for the rapid identification and promotion of new suppliers. My accounting background is applicable to bidding, estimating, and contract negotiations.

Moreover, I demonstrate extensive troubleshooting in sales, manufacturing and quality assurance and have performed market analyses for effective product promotions. I routinely deliver stand-up presentations to key decision makers to close multi-million dollar proposals. Further, my communication skills include fluency in English, German, and French.

An interview will allow me to discuss in greater detail how my background and experience, as well as my ability to adapt quickly to new settings, can assist you in accomplishing your business objectives.

Sincerely,

John Work

JOHN WORK
1150 Dancer Drive
Upland, CA 91786
(714) 949-1000

Qualifications

o Over 20 years progressive experience in management with particular emphasis on international sales and purchasing activities.

o Operational expertise includes profit and loss accountability, budgeting, forecasting and projecting for enhanced fiscal control.

o Can readily open new accounts, service existing transactions, open new territories and launch specialized brands through strategic marketing analyses and product promotions.

o Accounting expertise encompasses payables, receivables, collections, bidding, estimating, and contract negotiations for improved product integrity and customer relations.

o Supervision experience is demonstrated through scheduling, manpower planning, policy initiation and staff training for improved performance, productivity and commitment.

o Significant international exposure to identify and promote new suppliers, initiate purchasing activities, as provide logistical field support.

o Extensive troubleshooting and problem solving skills pertinent to sales, manufacturing and quality assurance for improved account revenue.

o Stand-up presentation proficiency to key decision makers, includes multi-million dollar proposals and strategic trade shows.

o Fluency in English, German, French, and Latin supported by outstanding oral and written communication skills

Education

ALFRED VOCATIONAL TRADE SCHOOL
Specialization: Business Administration.

ALFRED COMMERCIAL TRADE SCHOOL
Specialization: Business Administration.

Program emphasized such pertinent business areas as Accounting, Management, Personnel, Production, Manufacturing, Marketing, Organization, Logistics, International Trade, International Banking, and Social Dynamics.

Dr. Lawrence Peterson

Professional Experience

GLOSSEN PAPER, INCORPORATED

Sales Manager for one of the three largest paper wholesalers in Europe, represented by a highly diversified range of products, from raw materials to converted products in both sheet and roll stock configurations. Responsibilities included identifying and cultivating suppliers throughout the world for product sales to Germany, Switzerland and Austria. Apply technical troubleshooting to marketing activities to open new accounts and service existing transactions.

Position involves extensive public relations for the creation of new product outlets and applications, encompassing such business transactions as procurement, manufacturing, warehousing and shipping. Marketing initiatives included demographic analysis and pricing, as well as trade show development and presentations to key decision makers for enhanced product visibility and demand. Personnel functions involve hiring, evaluating, and training of personnel for enhanced performance, productivity and commitment. Endeavors resulted in over $20 million in annual sales.

RAPA INTERNATIONAL

Sales Manager for this international sales organization representing twenty paper mills throughout Europe with annual revenue in excess of $20 million. Responsibilities included sales to Germany, Austria, Switzerland and the East Bloc. Particular activities included market research, manufacturing, production, inventory control, warehousing, and distribution. Was recognized for outstanding sales performance.

ROPA RECYCLING

Regional Manager for the largest paper waste and recycling company in Europe. Responsibilities included commercial, technical and logistical support to enhanced performance, productivity and organizational efficiency. Specific activities encompassed sales, manufacturing, purchasing, warehousing, shipping and receiving, as well as extensive troubleshooting and problem solving.

Certification

Chamber of Commerce Award for Business Achievement Intermediate Examination for Common and Commercial English.

Dr. Lawrence Peterson

JACK M. BOSWELL
111 Box Street
Upland, CA 91786
(714) 949-0003

Thank you for the opportunity to present my Sales and Marketing expertise for your consideration.

A summary of my qualifications includes augmenting regional market share through the management of five distributor organizations encompassing 20 sales representatives. I routinely provide strategic field troubleshooting support to identify and correct account deficiencies for enhanced retention, repeat sales and referrals. I also attend distributor sales calls and have proven my ability to secure accounts, service existing transactions, open new territories, and launch specialized products and services.

My advertising, direct mail and telecommunications expertise is backed by trade show presentations to leverage leads into viable accounts. I am capable of servicing a large number of accounts as well as multiple product categories and can expedite field repairs for enhanced customer satisfaction. I also provide extensive distributor training while securing specialists for strategic product presentations to enhance product visibility and competitive sales awareness. Finally, my extensive electronic service experience is supported by digital electronic troubleshooting, project management experience, and field service exposure on both national and international levels.

An interview will allow me to discuss in greater detail how I can assist you in accomplishing your organizational objectives.

Sincerely,

Jack M. Boswell

Dr. Lawrence Peterson

JACK M. BOSWELL
111 Box Street
Upland, CA 91786
(714) 949-0003

Progressive experience in management supported by extensive sales and marketing expertise to generate additional account revenue and augment regional market share.

Successfully managed five distributor organizations encompassing 20 sales representatives, providing strategic field support and marketing assistance for significant growth.

Operational competence includes sales forecasting, both monthly and annually, sales itineraries, and account administration to track leads and provide factory feedback on lead follow-up.

Comprehensive ability to secure accounts, service existing transactions, open new territories and launch specialized products and services.

Extensive troubleshooting and problem solving skills to rapidly identify and correct account dysfunctions for enhanced retention, repeat sales and referrals.

Demonstrated proficiency with market data analysis and demographics for improved penetration and effective client needs assessments.

Sound advertising, direct mail and telecommunications expertise is backed by trade show presentations to leverage leads into viable accounts.

Capable of servicing a large number of accounts as well as multiple product categories while interfacing with service to expedite field repairs for enhanced customer satisfaction.

High energy personality who can interface with individuals

from diverse cultural backgrounds on a national and international level for enhanced cooperation and rapport.

Staff training and development abilities include securing specialists for strategic distributor presentations for enhance product visibility and competitive sales characteristics.

Extensive electronics service experience is supported by digital electronics troubleshooting, project management experience, and field service exposure.

Able to adapt quickly to new organizational settings and can leverage current client account base into new sales.

Education

Numerous trainings in sales by Carl Henry, and in grinding principles with Dr. Stewart Salmon, in addition to factory instruction with Jones and Shipman in England.

CONTROL DATA INSTITUTE, Los Angeles, CA Certificate, Computer Technology
750 class hours -150 hands-on hours, as well as seminars in computers.

JACK M. BOSWELL

Experience

BAXTER MACHINES, New York, NY
Present: Over twenty years' experience with this sales and service organization offering micro processed controlled grinding machine products to the United States and Canada.

As a Regional Sales Manager, set up the west coast distribution network to escalate sales from $ 1/2 million to approximately $ 2 million through strong commitment to existing and newly selected distributors. Manage 5 distributor organizations encompassing 20 sales representatives. Position necessitates extensive distributor training. Secure specialists for strategic seminar presentations to enhance product visibility and competitive product features over other products.

Routinely perform extensive troubleshooting and problem solving to rapidly identify and correct account dysfunctions for enhanced customer satisfaction, repeat sales and referrals. Apply analytical decision making proficiency to bid proposals, contract negotiations and contract administration.

Attend sales calls with distributor sales representatives to provide marketing support and lend technical assistance. Interface with service to expedite field repairs, while making factory recommendations for improved product reliability.

Expedite trade show presentations to convert leads into viable accounts. Call directly on accounts to secure additional account revenue. Follow-up on factory leads both personally and with sales representatives, providing factory feedback. Position necessitates extensive travel.
Prior position with company encompassed functioning as a Field Service Engineer where I applied strong technical analytical skills to the installation, repair and instruction of

basic operation and maintenance of field placed equipment, both nationally and internationally.

Dr. Lawrence Peterson

EDWARD K. LAYTON
800 Armstrong Street
Upland, CA 91786
(714) 935-9000

I am interested in applying for your position of Senior Marketing Representative where my technical background and marketing experience can satisfy U.S. and overseas military objectives.

My office experience is supported by senior management expertise in both aerospace and Air Force settings and I display work affiliation with such government agencies as PoP and NASA for strategic aerospace system development. I have provided input regarding future system modifications for significant increases in performance and cost effectiveness utilizing my troubleshooting skills to function as a liaison between customers and on-site facilities. My analytical decision making abilities allow for workable solutions to design, manufacturing and operational dysfunctions while my administrative competence includes budgeting, forecasting, and projecting.

Moreover, my procurement and manufacturing expertise includes the ability to service a large number of accounts and multiple product categories. I exhibit master scheduling and manpower planning skills for the maximization of capital and human resources and can readily apply my well-developed oral and written communication expertise for effective stand-up presentations.

An interview will allow me to discuss in greater detail how I can assist you in accomplishing your marketing objectives.

Sincerely,

Edward K. Layton

Dr. Lawrence Peterson

EPWARD R. LAYTON
800 Armstrong Street
Upland, CA 91786
(714) 985-9000

Military Marketing specialist seeks increased responsibility in a DoD environment.

o Program office experience firmly supported by senior management expertise in both aerospace and Air Force settings.

o Work affiliation with such government agencies as PoP and NASA for strategic aerospace system development.

o Provide input regarding future system modifications for significant increases in performance and cost effectiveness.

o Troubleshooting skills are complemented by liaison activities between customers and on-site facilities, resulting in enhanced organizational efficiency.

o Sound analytical decision making abilities for the development of workable solutions to design, manufacturing and operational dysfunctions.

o Responsible administrative competence is supported by such fiscal experience as budgeting, forecasting, and projecting.

o Procurement and manufacturing expertise includes the ability to service a large number of accounts and multiple product categories.

o Personnel skills include hiring, training, development, and employee performance appraisals.

o Master scheduling and manpower planning abilities for the maximization of capital and human resources.

o Outstanding oral and written communication skills with stand-up presentation expertise.

o PoP security clearance with EH for Special Access,

o Able to adapt quickly to new organizational settings.

Education

CALIFORNIA STATE UNIVERSITY, Dominguez Hills, CA Masters of business Administration in business Administration.

5T. LOUIS UNIVERSITY, St. Louis, MO bachelor of Science Degree in Aeronautics.
Numerous workshops and seminars on Technical and Management courses as well as college teaching experience.

License

Commercial Pilot - 4000 USAF Navigation hours and over 2000 Commercial Pilot ASMEL hours

EDWARD R. LAYTON

T.R.W., Space and Defense. Redondo Beach, CA

Assistant Project Manager responsible for satisfying a variety of on-going program initiatives encompassing Quality Assurance, Reliability, System Safety and Configuration Management on major DoD and NASA satellite programs. Prepared numerous proposals for satellite systems and associated ground equipment while interfacing with government program office representatives relative to the overall performance of deliverable systems. Activities Included proposal development in response to the RFP and the SOW. Initiated program plans, conducted submittal presentations, and responded to government fact-finding sessions. Also substantiated estimates during contract negotiations.

Developed subcontractors for subsystem hardware and investigated problems associated with sub-contractor and in-house manufactured hardware. Resolved electromechanical hardware problems through corrective action plans. Monitored unit subsystem and system integration inspections along with testing and documentation for customer briefings entailing system integrity for delivery and operational use. Conducted periodic briefings and prepared reports to government program office personnel on system status toward meeting system delivery dates. Also established and maintained control of $5 Million annual budget in accordance with government contract C-SPEC requirements. Hired and supervised approximately 100 direct and indirect personnel including technical and administrative staff members.

Other company held positions Included Quality Assurance Manager responsible for Quality Control of hi-res electronic and mechanical hardware. As Staff Manager of the Group Assurance Audits Office, directed planning, conducted system audits, reported results and ensured implementation of corrective actions. Functioned as a Staff Engineer to prepare technical program plans and cost estimates for spacecraft proposals. Also held various field positions for preparing and launching rocket propulsion vehicles in addition to preparing service manuals, bulletins and handbooks for maintaining, servicing and repairing aircraft systems.

Prior experience includes Mobilization Augmented to the Chief of Safety, Air Force Inspection and Safety Center; Colonel, USAF, Retired; USAF Navigator, 4000 hours, bomber and transport aircraft; and General Aviation Aircraft Salesman.

PAUL K. WALTER
16000 James Street
Upland, CA 91786
(714) 949-1082

Thank you for the opportunity to present an outline of my qualifications. In addition to possessing seven years' experience in Respiratory Therapy Care, a summary of my qualifications includes specialized knowledge in neonatal intensive care as well as various adult and pediatric modalities. I routinely provide strategic recommendations for new equipment to enhance neonatal care and have conducted in-service trainings for physicians, nurses, new staff therapists and students on new equipment applications.

Moreover, I demonstrate the ability to function effectively in pressure situations while exhibiting team leadership to foster enhanced performance and commitment to healthcare initiatives. My well-developed oral and written communication skills result in enhanced rapport and cooperation with affiliated medical personnel. Finally, I display prior marketing experience pertinent to new account development. Furthermore, I have participated in an on-going research project for billing and physiological data recording, along with subsequent analysis for enhanced compliance with insurance requirements.

An interview will allow me to discuss in greater detail how my background and experience, in addition to my ability to adapt quickly to new settings, can assist you in accomplishing your healthcare objectives.

Sincerely,

Paul K. Walter, CCIP, OPT

PAUL K. WALTER
16000 James Street
Upland, CA 91786
(714) 949-1082

Respiratory Therapist

o Possess specialized knowledge in neonatal intensive care in addition to various adult and pediatric modalities.

o Routinely provide strategic recommendations for equipment and therapeutic applications resulting in improved cardiopulmonary status.

o Well-developed oral and written communication skills for enhanced rapport and cooperation with clients and affiliated medical personnel.

o Can identify potential equipment applications for enhanced neonatal care as well as provide in-service training for physicians, nurses, new staff therapists and students on new equipment applications.

o Demonstrate the ability to function effectively in pressure situations while exhibiting team leadership to foster enhanced performance and commitment to healthcare initiatives.

o Marketing experience includes the ability to open new accounts as well as service existing accounts.

Education

UNIVERSITY CE CALIFORNIA - RIVERSIDE, Riverside, CA Specialization: Biology Scholastic Leadership Scholarship.

MOUNT SAN ANTONIO COLLEGE, Walnut, CA Specialization: Respiratory Therapist Program A.S. in Respiratory Therapy, Dean's Honor List.

CHAFFEY COMMUNITY COLLEGE, Alta Loma, CA A.S. in Biology. Dean's Honor List.

PAUL K. WALTER
16000 James Street
Upland, CA 91786
(714) 949-1082

INLAND VALLEY MEDICAL CENTER
Neonatal Respiratory Care Practitioner

In addition to serving as a member of the Transport and Neonatal Resuscitation Team, routinely respond to all neonatal codes, C-sections and high risk deliveries. Administer aerosolized, intratracheal and intramuscular medications, and such mechanically ventilated airway management as endotracheal intubations. Other activities include CBG/ABG sampling and analysis, CPR, transcutaneous CO2, O2, and saturation monitoring. Exogenous Surfactant administration.

Equipment: Sechrist Infant Ventilator, Infant Star Ventilator, Corning ABG analyzer, high flow oxygen and humidity delivery systems.

PROGRESSIVE PEDIATRICS, INCORPORATED
Respiratory Care Practitioner-Field Representative/Patient Manager

Instruct parents in the use of apnea monitors, oxygen delivery, aerosol therapy, ventilators and feeding pumps, as well as CPR training. Conduct pnuemocar-diograms, polysomnograms, and oximetry studies. Provide on-going follow-up regarding patient contracts for continued patient monitoring and clinical updates. Meet with referral centers/provider groups for current updates in discharge planning. Provide in-service training to physicians and nurses on new durable medical equipment.

Equipment: Aequitron 9200, 9500, 9550, Edentech 2000W and 2000W Memory Module, Corometrics 500E Apnea Monitors, PB2800 and Lifecare LP4 Ventilators, Aequitron 9100

Pneumogram Recording System and Edentrace 4 Channel Recording System, Devilbiss Pulmoaides and Corometrics Kangaroo Pumps.

MODERN II IRAPy SERVICES, INCORPORATED
Respiratory Care Practitioner-Field Representative/Patient Manager

Responsible for Pediatric Respiratory Home Care, including instructing parents in the use of Apnea Monitors, ventilators, pulmoaides, compressors and home oxygen, as well as CPR procedures. Recorded and transmitted two-channel pneumograms. Provided on-going follow-up through patient contacts for continued patient monitoring and clinical updates.

Equipment: Aequitron 8200/9200 Apnea Monitors, PB-2800/LP-4 Ventilators, PCS-4 Compressors, Two-Channel Pneumograms - Oxford Recorder, Aequitron 8100/9100.

BRIEN L. COOPER
10000 Gaunt Avenue
Upland, CA 91786
(714) 949-1682

Thank you for the opportunity to present an outline of my qualifications. I am a Management specialist who presently seeks increased responsibility in a challenging environment where my diverse background can be efficiently applied to the satisfaction of organizational objectives.

A summary of my qualifications includes seasoned management experience supported by a track record for significantly improving operational efficiency. My operational expertise includes budgeting, forecasting and auditing proficiency pertinent to virtually all operational areas, from accounting to distribution. I routinely provide troubleshooting support to rapidly diagnose and remedy operational dysfunctions while effectively interfacing with management, key decision makers and affiliated personnel to clarify and further organizational policies.

Moreover, I have served as a resource person for new account development and security system analysis, and have consistently demonstrated my ability for functioning effectively in pressure situations to meet crisis situations. I am also capable of hiring, scheduling, evaluating, training and motivating staff personnel for enhanced performance, productivity and organizational commitment. Finally, my communication skills are supported by staff meetings and newsletter article initiation to promote awareness to security initiatives.

An interview will allow me to discuss in greater detail how my background and experience, in addition to my ability to adapt quickly to new settings, can assist you in accomplishing your organizational objectives.

Sincerely,

Brien L. Cooper

BRIEN L. COOPER
10000 Gaunt Avenue
Upland, CA 91786
(714)949-1682

Management specialist seeks increased responsibility in a challenging environment where background can be efficiently applied to the satisfaction of organizational objectives.

Summary of Qualifications

o Extensive experience in management supported by a track record for significantly improving operational efficiency and security integrity.

o Comprehensive operational expertise includes budgeting, forecasting, projecting, cash and inventory control, as well as security audits pertinent to distribution and merchandising.

o Extensive troubleshooting and problem solving skills to rapidly diagnose and remedy operational and organizational dysfunctions.

o Demonstrated interface proficiency with management, key decision makers and affiliated personnel to further organizational policies and objectives.

o Sound analytical decision making abilities supported by seasoned documentation and contract administration.

o Have served as a resource person for new account development, security system analysis and procedure clarification.

o Consistently able to function effectively in pressure situations to meet scheduled deadlines as well as to expediently handle crisis situations.

o Capable of hiring, scheduling, evaluating, training and motivating staff personnel for enhanced performance, productivity and organizational commitment.

o Experience managing large projects as well as multiple assignments simultaneously with emphasis on quality, safety and project integrity.

o Well-developed oral and written communication skills are supported by staff meetings and French facility.

Education

CALIFORNIA STATE POLYTECHNIC UNIVERSITY, Pomona, CA Specialization: Political Science - Pre Law.

MOUNT SAN ANTONIO COMMUNITY COLLEGE, Walnut, CA Associate of Arts Degree: Business Administration.

Additional instruction in Management by Objectives, Executive Training, Loss Prevention, Shortage Control, Security Management, and Personnel Administration.

BRIEN L. COOPER

Professional Experience

ALARM SYSTEMS, Upland, CA
Occupied such positions as Customer Service Manager, Major Accounts Manager, and Central Station Manager. Diverse activities included developing the company's Customer Service Program, Major Accounts and National Sales Departments, requiring policy and procedure initiation, staff supervision and interface with such organizations as Coca Cola, Sav-On, Bullocks, Bergen-Brunswick, and Arrowhead, resulting in an annually recurring revenue in excess of $6 million. Staffed and managed one of the largest and most modern, computerized alarm company central stations. Contributed significantly to the development of a MIS program, providing maximum analysis of customer data, account tracking and management response. Initiated a large scale conversion program, subsequently implemented on a company-wide basis for a savings of $3 million.

Participated in the development of the corporate philosophy and occupied a key role in the Corporate Training Program, functioning as instructor for areas related to Negotiations, Business Writing, Alarm Equipment, Security Policies and Procedures. Participated in top level contract negotiations and legal positioning while boasting the highest customer retention record in the organization. Other activities included troubleshooting and problem solving support to rapidly identify and correct security dysfunctions. Interface with internal API personnel to schedule customer calls and generate effective needs assessments. Provided staff meetings at Corporate offices relative to accounting for all products and services. Also performed budgeting and forecasting. Personnel skills encompassed hiring, scheduling, training and performance evaluations. Authored numerous articles in the company newsletter. Position necessitated strong documentation abilities in addition to effective performance in stressful situations.

THE FEDERAL GROUP, Upland, CA
Began with company as a Corporate Auditor responsible for the design, installation and audit of security systems and procedures relative to store operations, shrinkage, inventory control, shipping, receiving, warehousing and distribution. Was rapidly promoted to Loss Prevention and Security Manager with responsibility for directing managers in such initiatives as loss prevention, merchandise control and appropriate documentation procedures for ten branch locations employing over 450 staff personnel. Conducted weekly staff meetings to enhance conformance to stated security objectives.

Additional Reading:

Transformational Job Strategies for Getting the Job You Want.

Lawrence Frederick Peterson Ph.D., 2012, Amazon, Kindle.

Return to TOC